WHAT DIFFERENCE
DOES IT MAKE?

WHAT DIFFERENCE DOES IT MAKE?

What Happened to our Country

BELLA T ALTURA

TABLE OF CONTENTS

PROLOGUE

Let me introduce myself. I am a proud American citizen who loves this country with all her heart, having come to it after ten years of yearning to be saved. I have had the priceless gift of making a good life for myself through this country's good graces, the wonders of freedom, and infinite opportunities.

In that other life, I spent my adult years in golden America. I was a scientist looking to impart health and well-being by studying basic facts in one little corner of the human condition, and together with my life partner, I was successful in coming up with some helpful answers. Now, mostly retired, I am an old lady who has made it her calling to give back to this country something of what I received. I want to help it be what it was all those many years I sojourned here when I was happy, contented, and sure I was safe.

I am no political pundit or learned historian who can talk authoritatively on the subject but is removed from it by way of being wrapped in a bubble of elitism and scholarship. What I do bring to the table is common sense. I see with my eyes, hear with my ears, and integrate what is in front of me using reason and logic. In addition, I sense what is proper and right and can compare that with what is not.

Those are my qualifications to write this book. You may say that is hardly a recommendation for you to read it. But I would suggest then that you try. You might like it. And if not, you can always discard it afterward and have the privilege of becoming a critic.

I do have to warn the reader that I am a stickler for details by training. I like to show facts and truths, point by point, so that what I say becomes clear and self-evident.

Also, I trust the reader to be sophisticated enough about current events that, if I mention Syria, Iran, or ISIS, he or she knows what I am talking about.

Let us then embark on this journey. I have taken the liberty of adding some personal notes in parenthesis when I needed to vent or make a particularly important point. I start the story close to the present time, beginning on a positive note (for the relief of a heavy burden of anxiety) and go to the disturbing past later.

Chapter 1

ONE HUNDRED DAYS AFTER
THE 2017 INAUGURATION

It is a bright and sunny day. The sky is a perfect blue; not a cloud is to be seen. The day will be hot, but now a gentle breeze plays with the palm tree branches and cools the air just enough to make it feel like a warm and cozy blanket. I step out on the lanai and proceed into the pool to do my usual sixty laps. I am elated. Burt, my husband, confessed to me last night that he feels happy—happy to sometimes live in this paradise, happy to be able to pursue his work, and happy that we have just barely dodged the final fatal bullet in the election and put Donald Trump in the White House.

Today is the one hundredth day since our new president's inauguration. He has been working steadily ever since he got elected, even before he was inaugurated, day after day, seemingly needing very little sleep, to bring this country back from the brink of disaster. It seems an impossible job. The progressive jackals are a constant encumbrance around his neck. Every word he says they vilify; every step he takes, they immediately act to stop. Yet he has succeeded in many tasks already, despite the left's incessant distribution of evil through the mainstream media and its full-time scheming obstruction and distraction, helped by the liberal judges the previous administration put in place.

He wants to prevent illegal immigration from ISIS-friendly countries, but a lefty judge prevents him from going ahead. He wants to stop financing sanctuary cities, but a progressive judge disallows it. What I don't understand is that these lefties do not see that they put themselves, their families and friends, and the whole country in danger. How can they be so blind? It is a puzzlement (an expression I borrow from Yul Brynner, which he used in *The King and I*, a wonderful musical whose story and music I always enjoy).

At ten o'clock I meet some Republican friends at the intersection of two large highways to hold a sort of rally. We stand near the busy streets in our Trump hats and shirts and wave our country's flag, holding signs saying "Make America Great Again," "I Love Trump and Pence, signed A Deplorable," "Women for Trump," and "Veterans for Trump." We urge the many passing drivers to honk their horns. One of us has a bullhorn and is addressing the occupants of cars that stop for the red lights, saying "Unite, don't fight, Unite, don't fight," or we all chant "USA, USA." It is a labor of love, even in the ninety-degree heat that is making us sweat and drink water by the gallon, but we stay for the full three hours we planned. We are happy to do it, happy to do anything we can to show our deep appreciation for having this miracle man at our helm.

Before we leave we promise one another we will do this again on the two-hundred-day anniversary, but next time, we will bring larger signs and encourage more friends to join us. We depart for our homes, but we remind one another not to forget to show up at our regular Republican club meeting next Thursday. There is a wonderful camaraderie among us; we are all of one mind and know one another even if we have never met before. We are the deplorable, irredeemable Trumpsters, and we know what we stand for. We stand for faith, we stand for morals and ethics, we stand for law and order, and we are committed to upholding the Constitution. We are filled with

American patriotism in our hearts and God in our souls, and we want to help make our America great again.

This afternoon, after some rest, I get ready to listen to the speech the president will make in Harrisburg, Pennsylvania, to celebrate his one-hundredth day in office. He has decided to go to Pennsylvania, a blue state for years, but much of its population voted for him and thus helped him win the election. Trump does not forget; he thanks his supporters every chance he gets. The speech will be delivered at seven thirty, but I sit in front of my TV starting at six o'clock to make sure the TV is warmed up and to ensure I don't miss anything. The facility in Pennsylvania is filled to capacity. There are people galore. Everywhere folks are holding up big flags and big signs, such as "Women for Trump," "Veterans for Trump," "Make America Great Again," and "Blacks for Trump." It is a pleasure to behold, and I feast my eyes on this spectacle.

At around seven o'clock, Vice President Michael Pence comes to the podium to great clapping and welcoming shouts. He yells, "Hello, Pennsylvania. It is great to be back." Then he tells us in his usual calm manner, "Our president is a man of action, and he has been keeping his words. He is a tireless leader despite the left fake news. Our country is back. Our jobs are back. He has been slashing through the red tape and signed orders for the Keystone Pipeline and the Dakota Pipeline, for offshore drilling and energy independence, and the war on coal is over. He intends to cut taxes for middle-class families, farmers, and small businesses. He has made trade deals that places us first, and he will repeal and replace Obamacare. He has created five hundred thousand new jobs for us. He wants jobs for us in our businesses, and this has created optimism and confidence, exactly what he promised to do. President Trump has signed more good laws in his one hundred days than any other president before him. He is led by the Constitution, upholds the Second Amendment, and has replaced the conservative Supreme Court Justice Antonin Scalia (deceased under suspicious circumstances) with another young conservative constitutionalist. He has stood by law enforcement, already secured the borders much better than they were, as illegal entry is down by seventy percent. He has given more resources to the military by increased defense spending and helped our veterans get world-class health care. We are standing with our allies, and he has put Iran and North Korea on notice as well as putting ISIS on the run in Iran, Syria, and Afghanistan. In one hundred days, he has turned our country around, and he is just getting started. We will make America great again."

At this point President Trump comes to the podium, and everybody stands up and shouts, "USA, USA." Both Trump and Pence clap their hands. It is a heartwarming moment, and I have tears running down my cheeks.

After the live audience of about twelve thousand people quiets down, the president says, "A large group of Hollywood actors and Washington media are consoling each other in a hotel ballroom right now. They are gathered together for the White House Correspondents Dinner—without the president." Loud boos are heard, and he continues. "And I could not possibly be more thrilled than to be one hundred miles away from Washington spending my evening with all of you, a much larger crowd and much better people…Media outlets like CNN and MSNBC are fake news…But they're trapped at the dinner…We are just beginning in our fight to make America great again…

"Let's rate the media's one hundred days…Because, as you know, they are a disgrace…More than half of Americans say the media is 'out of touch with everyday Americans'…Eighty-nine percent of the media's coverage of our administration has been negative…Ninety-six percent of journalists who made donations in the last election gave to our opponent… According to a poll last year from the Associated Press, only six percent of Americans have a lot of confidence in America [sic]."

So just as an example of fake media, take the *New York Times*. Pretty soon, they'll only be on the Internet. They sold their *New York Times* building for one hundred thirty million dollars. A group that bought it later sold it for five hundred million. And now they live in an unassuming building. They had to apologize because their predictions were so wrong.

I quietly say, "Thank God."

Now after this slight mocking of the media and the other side, President Trump gets to the work at hand—telling us all he has accomplished. He has already eliminated some terrible job regulations to put the miners, steel workers, and aluminum workers back to work. He tells us rightly that the previous administration gave us a mess. (That is the understatement of the century.) It produced job theft by other countries and illegals and caused an unbelievable seventy thousand of our American factories to close down. He tells us that the open borders result in gangs flooding in, there is no safety in our country, and we pay foreign workers for our goods. He tells us that in the Paris Accord, regarding global warming, we pay. China, Russia, and India, the countries that pollute the most, pay nothing. The Iran deal is the worst deal ever made, and we are totally unsafe from within and without. We are losing jobs by the hundreds of thousands. Yet none of these facts are reported in the media. He says the Democrats' agenda is not our agenda; it is a global theft of our wealth. Now we will put America first.

To give an example of the fake news, he explains that though he called China a currency manipulator while campaigning, he just met with the president of China in the White House and asked him to help us with the threat of North Korea. The two leaders got along well, and it seems that China is now helping us with that problem by putting some of its military on the Korean border and by no longer buying Korean coal, but buying it from us instead. The media reported repeatedly that Trump was not keeping his word by not mentioning the currency manipulation while China's president was in the White House. How dumb would that have been, Trump says, to criticize China's president when we needed him to help us?

Trump turns back to his one hundred days of action. He tells us that he has exhausted his administration with his stamina and work ethic.

It is an amazing thing, a wonder to behold. It comes through clearly as he speaks. In the way he goes from one topic to another, we can see how many different causes he is pursuing at the same time. I have to contain my amazement not to miss a word of what he says. He has worked steadily to:

1) bring back jobs,
2) allow offshore drilling,
3) eradicate criminal gangs and cartels and cancel what does not protect us. He has:
4) created a foundation of understanding with Germany, Japan, China, and the United Kingdom.
5) put a new justice on the Supreme Court who will uphold the Constitution and boasts this had not been done by any president in the first one hundred days for 136 years.
6) withdrawn from TPP, the Trans Pacific Partnership, (a pact between 11 countries and the US, where we would essentially pay and they would benefit) a deal that would have been a disaster for America. He launches into the fact that there has been steel and aluminum dumping from abroad, which prevented us from selling and using our own. He promises to:
7) review NAFTA, The North American Free Trade Agreement, (a pact between Canada, Mexico and the USA, where we again get the short end of the stick) with the commerce secretary and renegotiate it if it can be done to be fair to all countries concerned.

He reminds us that the state of Pennsylvania would benefit, as it has steel factories that would be revived.

His plan is to buy American goods and hire American workers. He has so far:

8) created six hundred thousand new jobs, among them twenty-seven thousand coal miner jobs, and by removing the shackles on oil, shale, and gas and allowing the pipelines to go forward, he has created forty-eight thousand new jobs in the energy industry.

9) scrapped the job-killing regulations for auto workers and construction workers.

President Trump has decided to enforce the edict that:

10) for each new regulation put forth, two old ones have to be eliminated, thus stopping the red tape of intrusive federal regulations.

The president has mandated that:

11) all veterans who cannot get health care from the Veterans Administration within a reasonable amount of time be allowed to use their VA benefits to access private care, which 42 percent are now doing. He has also established an office of accountability at the VA.

He has stipulated that:

12) no congressperson can become a lobbyist for five years after his or her retirement, and retired congresspersons are banned from ever lobbying for a foreign government.

With the loudest applause and shouted approval, the president announces "It is time to drain the swamp" and " Oh, don't worry, we're going to have the wall. Don't worry about it." He adds my favorite phrase he often uses: "Believe me." We need the wall, he says, to stop drugs from poisoning our children, to end human trafficking, and to screen people coming in. It is now American citizens first.

There is already:

13) a 73 percent reduction in illegal crossing, and we have just started.

He says, "We will protect American lives."

He has, he says:

14) opened an office to support victims who have suffered from crimes committed by illegals. He reiterates we need safety and the wall to stop crimes; drugs; and monstrous, mean gangs like the MS-13 from coming into our country. The gang members have wreaked havoc in Long Island schools, where he himself grew up safe and sound, as well as in all fifty states. He then points to the minority leader of the Senate as being a bad leader because his policies are hurting America. (That, too, is the understatement of the century.) He—Senator Charles E. Schumer—wants taxes to go up, leading the Democrats to doom (more about that later).

The president wants to restore the rule of law and fight sanctuary cities that shield criminals from being removed from our country. To support the rule of law, he signed an executive order allowing Attorney General Jefferson B. Sessions to combat crimes against the police, keep us safe from terrorism, and improve visa vetting so we don't allow in those who want to kill Americans.

The president then reads the lyrics of a song titled "The Snake" by Oscar Brown. (See appendix.) It fits well with his desire to prevent radical Islamic terrorists coming into the United States and to step up the fight against ISIS. He continues, underlining his will to rebuild the military and restore readiness.

He reveals that he was:

15) able to save $425 million on new planes by haggling with the builders.

He then tells us that he has:

16) brought home an American woman who was to be jailed for twenty-eight years in a prison in Egypt and another eight prisoners. He accomplished this feat by speaking to Egyptian President Abdel Fattah el-Sisi for one minute, while the former POTUS could not get it done in three and a half years. (I wonder if he even tried, there being no gain in it for his agenda.)

He has worked to cut taxes so that the middle class can keep more of their money, and businesses have the possibility of expanding and hiring more people. He has instructed Congress to repeal and replace the unaffordable and dying Obamacare, in which premiums increased substantially and deductibles are much too high. In fact, many insurance carriers refuse to continue selling health insurance in some states, and one half the people living in the state of Tennessee are already without insurance.

It is the president's intention, he says, to allow American citizens to have the health insurance they want, to give back power to the people where it belongs, to keep the Second Amendment intact, and to end Common Core (the latter, an unbelievably bad teaching curriculum, in which our history has been rewritten so as not to be recognized, simple arithmetic has been turned into a complicated series of computations, and students are given multiple tests every week, paid for by tax payers, to applaud the good work of the teachers.) Loud and persistent cheers rise from the audience. He intends to give education back to the states, to give back the hope of safety, to instill into children pride in our flag, and to get back the respect we deserve from other countries.

He finishes his speech with the following: "It's time for us all to remember that we are one people, with one great American destiny… we all bleed the same red blood of patriots. And we all share the same glorious freedoms of our magnificent country. We are all made by the same Almighty God. As long as we remember these truths, we will not fail…The future belongs to us… I say these words to you tonight, on one hundred days of devotion, hard work and love for our great country: Together we will make America strong again. We will make America wealthy again. We will make America prosper again. We will make America proud again. We will make America safe again. And we will make America great again."

I stood up from my chair and clapped repeatedly along with the people watching live in Harrisburg. Then I turned off the TV to avoid having to hear the pundits' take on the president's speech, every word of which I had savored and enjoyed.

So, he has accomplished sixteen of the promises he made during his candidacy, and here it is only three months since he officially started to be our president.

I knew most of what he had said, as I follow politics every day by listening to my favorite commentators, like Sean Hannity, Lou Dobbs, Stewart Varney, Rush Limbaugh, Mark Levin, and a few others. I also get input from conservative Internet sources and Burt's daily ruminations from reading the *Wall Street Journal*, the *New York Post*, the *Washington Times*, the *Financial Times of London*, the local papers, Breitbart News, and the Drudge Report. He keeps me informed about all important matters as the first thing out of my mouth every morning is "What's new?"

It is his habit to inform himself early in the morning, getting up with the birds, and late at night by perusing—much to my chagrin—the five or six newspapers he buys daily, the umpteen papers and journals he gets through the mail, and the Internet sites he follows religiously. It's not that I am not grateful for all the information he gathers and gladly imparts to me, but papers, magazines, and journals are in every nook and cranny of our home, growing steadily in very neat piles. (He tells me that he likes to hold on to important information, and he keeps some to read and enjoy at his leisure when he has more time.) Even our kitchen is fair game. When I blow up once in a while, he will move some piles from the top of the kitchen table to a chair in the dining room that is not so glaringly visible and say, "See what I do for you?" What can I do but grin and bear it? I am so lucky to get my information from an infinitely credible source in an infinitely easy way. Burt is blessed with a photographic memory that never, or almost never, lets him down. (But I digress.)

It is most amazing how our president can go from one topic to another, constantly working and constantly moving forward to implement as many of the promises he made as a candidate as possible, in effect checking off items from a list he prepared during his campaign.

THE JACKALS

But the mainstream media, the Democratic pundits, and the lefty constituents are strongly resisting the plain truth. The minority leader of the House and the minority leader of the Senate boldly go on record as saying that here it is one hundred days into Trump's presidency, and he has not accomplished a single thing! There is an incredible hatred that has developed in the past eight years of the previous administration. It has settled among the so-called progressive Democrats and remained in place in their minds, a crass compulsion that has invaded their subconscious, resulting in the firm belief that whatever the conservatives do is hateful and untrue. This mantra has become a religion that has taken hold of the Democrats. One has to call it brainwashing for lack of any other way to explain it. Whatever the president does 1) is no good for the country, 2) is no good for the American people, and 3) simply does not exist.

It is a phenomenon that I cannot understand. I often ask my friends and neighbors how it is possible that people who seem intelligent and are functioning and holding down jobs can be so dense as not to see with their eyes and hear with their ears facts right in front of them. Instead they respond like Pavlov's dogs. They spew out whatever lies they heard from the mainstream media and indulge in the hate they have nurtured listening to one another. They repeat the same phrases to one another, internalized from the mainstream media, like a bunch of robots. What is interesting to see is that whichever lefty is interviewed, be it a congressperson, a Democratic leader, or a lefty citizen, the same phrases come out. If it is light outside and a conservative observes it in passing, they will insist it is dark. If something is insuring safety for our inhabitants that is obviously good for everybody, they will say it is dangerous and evil. If a health-care proposal will give us better care at lower prices, well, then they say it is going to kill hundreds of thousands of people. (Honestly, I have heard it myself repeatedly.)

THE WORK GOES ON

This week, the president continues undeterred. He helps the House pass a continuing resolution through September 2017 so the government does not shut down and keeps on speaking to and telephoning House members to bring forward the repeal and replacement of Obamacare. In the same week, he is meeting with the Palestinian president. (He invited the Israeli prime minister a week or so ago.) He is trying to broker peace between Israel and the Palestinians, a daunting undertaking, as Palestinian children from the age of two onward are taught in school to hate Jews and to practice with knifes to kill them. It is well known that those families who do kill Jews or create havoc in Israel get special financial compensation. In addition, they name streets after and erect monuments to those terrorists who have succeeded in murdering Jews.

On the next day, he goes to New York to meet with the premier of Australia on the *Intrepid*, an aircraft carrier that was involved in a decisive battle fought in the Coral Sea seventy-five years ago, during World War II, preventing the Japanese from attacking Australia.

The following week, he is set to go on a trip to Saudi Arabia, Israel, the Vatican, Belgium, and Sicily to continue to act toward accomplishing peace and make some deals to further his job creation agenda, which has shown an increase of some twenty thousand in the last month and driven the Dow Jones Industrial Average farther up.

How he manages is beyond belief, but his speeches are all specific and to the point. The president keeps us all informed directly by weekly briefings through his press secretary, whose conferences are broadcast daily on Fox News, and by some early-morning tweets.

I love his tweets. When I was talking to a friend on Facebook, I received the following comment from her (AM):

The media only hates Trump tweeting because it is impossible to misquote him. He gives the world instant proof of exactly what he said (typed) with a time stamp indicating exactly when he said it. And he has more followers reading his posts, which get reposted and shared than any media outlet has viewers paying attention at any given time. Even better is the fact that for every "objectionable" tweet the president posts, which the media immediately draws attention to, there are 10–15 other good and positive Trump tweets that get just as much if not more attention and exposure. Unlike the newspapers and the TV crews, the media can't control or filter the information that Trump's followers have access to or share themselves.

That comment is so to the point.

Chapter 2

THE PREVIOUS ADMINISTRATION

It is now time to tackle the painful past eight years, the previous administration. We have the job of explaining how in heaven's name we got to a point, which was in my estimation a point of no return except for some miracle. Never in the many years since I immigrated legally and became an American citizen had I ever worried about this country remaining the one free unique haven I came to. How did it happen, in the previous eight years that I lost all hope and became depressed and dejected over the state of the union? Let us go to the videotape.

THE DISSOLUTION OF OUR BELOVED COUNTRY AND THE TRAMPLING ON OUR CONSTITUTION

I had been forewarned about the dangers of electing the last president by two commentators I listened to every weekday and Burt's reporting from his many readings; we knew full well not to vote for him. But in my worst nightmares I could never have imagined what happened in the last eight years. Had my compatriots been asleep at the wheel? Had they been paralyzed and unable to react to what was happening or in any way incapable of understanding what was in front of their eyes?

From the very first day after his inauguration, I became more and more appalled at what I saw and heard.

During his candidacy, the two news commentators I listened to daily during the week expounded repeatedly Barack Obama's background and qualifications for the presidency. He was the son of a Kenyan citizen, a Muslim, who remained in a marriage to a socialist-communist Caucasian lady for about three years, going back to the Kenyan wife he had never divorced. (It must not have been a great feeling having been abandoned by one's father at such a young age for little Barack.) Barry, his American name, had then been taken to Indonesia, where his stepfather, Lolo Soetoro, a Muslim, too, had adopted him and made sure he went to school and practiced his religion. After a while his mom sent her son back to the United States to be brought up by her parents. (I wonder what impact it has on one's ego to be abandoned by one parent and then the other, too.)

His grandparents, a fine white family, raised him. To avoid neglecting his indoctrination and at the same time give him a father figure to look up to, they provided him with a tutor, an African American communist, who took over the job of teaching him all things important to his credo. When he entered college, he did it as a minority student to help him become accepted easily to the school.

Before becoming a candidate for the highest post in the United States, Barack attended Occidental College, Columbia University, and Harvard Law School. At Harvard, he had been an instructor, but he called himself a scholar of the Constitution (lie number one). He then was a lecturer at the University of Chicago Law School. While there, he became a community organizer, urging people to come out and vote Democratic.

I have to pause here and explain the following important distinction of who he really was, much to the misperception of every Democrat, other progressives, and the American citizens. Barack Obama never was what we call an African American in the true meaning of the word. None of his ancestors were brought here as slaves—not a one. He is the first half African, half Caucasian of his family to be here, a free man with an African father who had spent a few years going to school in the United States and a white American mother. So, he may have some color but never the true identity of an African American person: that is, a descendant of slaves. Strangely, no one ever brought that up, but it is so plain and true. And all those voters who voted proudly for the first African American president deceived themselves and still are deceiving themselves about this truly so-called historical election.

Come to think of it, they all made a similar mistake when they eagerly voted for the first woman president. Hillary is far from being a woman in the real sense of the word, a caring, motherly type who would do anything to protect her children, give them the unconditional love they deserve, and make any sacrifice to protect her family, the American people. (But more about that later.)

Proceeding to law school, Barack met his wife, Michelle. The Reverend Wright married them in a church the candidate had attended for the past twelve years. The Reverend Wright had a pet mind-set that he used in his sermons. He was concerned with preaching about the sins of the American citizenry: owning slaves, committing the grave errors of capitalism, and, as he explained, "becoming rich on the backs of the poor." He often referred to white Americans as a greedy lot and proclaimed the disaster of 9/11 as the "chickens coming home to roost"—in other words, a well-deserved punishment. He was heard ending some sermon in the following manner: "No, no, not God bless America; it is God damn America." The candidate listened to those speeches for twelve years, but when some reporters mentioned that he had listened to such hate-filled sermons, Obama clearly explained that in all honesty, he had never heard such talk (lie number two).

His wife, on the other hand, exulted during the candidacy that she had never been proud of this country until now, her husband being a candidate for the presidency. This was an odd thing to say for one who had been accepted to the best schools and enjoyed every luxury available to an upper-middle-class family.

Now here the Democrats and many Republicans put a person in the White House who 1) was abandoned by his father and mother (a circumstance that has to have had severe character-impacting effects, no doubt); 2) was Muslim educated; 3) was taught the basics of communism as a child; 4) went to a church where the sermons repeatedly sought to punish America for its sin of becoming a rich and powerful country, which had given both the preacher and Barack's well-to-do family every luxury available; 5) was familiar with and had studied *Rules of Radicals*, a bible Saul Alinsky wrote that tells you all you need to know about how to subjugate your fellow country people and keep them poor and uneducated just to vote so you can continue to be the elite boss and follow your agenda, as became evident in his behavior; 6) had as best friends two unrepentant terrorists, in whose home he had announced his candidacy; and 7) was financed by a group of people whose chief was Satan himself.

If you think about all that, you have to shudder and predict that no good can come from such an unholy background. But it was impossible to foresee or understand what would really happen in the eight years of this person's administration. The professionalism of the disaster, how well it worked, and how smoothly it was executed in a country that had been all good, all law abiding, all reasonable.

(The only fault I had found to complain about before Mr. Obama's ascent to the White House was a leftover effect from the Clinton administration. This was the increasingly violent, unethical, and unsavory movies and television shows Hollywood was producing. I worried about the poison distributed to the minds of children and young adults. Fool that I was, I hoped that most people would do what I did and simply never watch any of these foul productions and that most parents would restrict TV viewing for their children. But often, that was not what occurred. Many young people took it all in and became desensitized to violence and bad behavior, sadly not learning what was humane and good.)

What happened right after the inauguration in 2009 was a systematic disassembling of our beloved country. Day after day, new abominations took place, a new trampling on our Constitution, a new usurping of our freedom. It was so obvious to see, but most people were blinded by the news media, which reported lies and distortions and omitted salient facts to suit the administration's agenda, the new order of the day. The majority of ordinary, hardworking, decent American citizens no longer mattered.

The mottoes during the 2008 election cycle had been "Hope and change" and "Change you can believe in." Change we can believe in—and nothing more. How clever this was; what a joke on every citizen. Oh yes, there were also three very appealing promises: 1) transparency; 2) no lobbyists in the new administration; and 3) the country coming together as never before.

GOVERNING BY OUR NEW LEADER: THE STIMULUS BILL

The first order of business after the election was to stimulate the economy and create jobs, since the economy had been on a downward roll. A bill was crafted—no one knows by whom—for which a sinful amount of money was to be taken from the taxpayer's fund. The bill was thousands of pages long, therefore the people who were to vote on it in a few days were unable to read it. But, oh yes, it was imperative that it be passed in the shortest amount of time or else there would be dire consequences of unimagined proportions to the economy, so said "the Anointed One," to borrow a name my favorite commentator coined. So, it was passed without being read and without being seen by the Congress people who had to vote it in. Nor was it read by the citizens. It resulted in short order in the liquidation of trillions of dollars, supposedly as a stimulus to create jobs, but instead the money was distributed to those who had helped with the election; and it became pork and more pork to friends. As a consequence, the economy went down further, and more jobs were lost. To summarize this first catastrophe (and there were many more to come), the bill was passed in the middle of the night and was too long to be read by any member of Congress, but the president kept repeating it had to be done quickly or things would get very much worse—so it passed.

That was the first of innumerable steps which followed day after day to continue the dissolution of our country with utter disregard of our cherished Constitution. The hurry to pass all these bills was so great that one could not take a breath before another abomination loomed on the horizon.

THE CAP-AND-TRADE BILL

The cap-and-trade bill was designed to combat human impact on global warming, a huge abomination. (It was designed to put a limit to the emission of carbon dioxide into the atmosphere and to buy from companies only, which manufacture such devices.) First off, the science of global warming is a feebleminded myth set forth by an unscrupulous layman and his cronies for the accumulation of unfathomable wealth at the expense of the innocent public. The unadulterated idiocy of inducing farmers to keep their cows from passing gas, citizens to use mercury-laden lightbulbs that need hazmat procedures to discard when broken and are twenty times more expensive than those that Thomas Edison left us, consumers to have wind-driven electricity, and drivers to use cars that run on ethanol or batteries is lunacy. Thinking that these things would really make a difference to the globe in the face of whole continents like Asia, South America and Africa is ridiculous. Countries like Russia and others are laughing at us and with good reason. The arrogance of thinking that those huge lands, third-world countries with dictators, warlords, and other unsavory leaders, would follow our example for whatever reason was enormously ludicrous. But just as ridiculous was our citizens' blindness if they believed the wicked fairy tale.

Then there was the urgent matter of ecology, the sacred duty to preserve all manner of animal and plant species for posterity as overseen by the EPA. As it was observed that little fish were on the verge of becoming extinct in a river in California, the EPA ordered the cutoff of the water supply of a whole valley there; farmers in a once-fertile land stood to live on food stamps—another example of vicious lunacy. Or was it more than that—a purposeful dispossession of the farmers' land to build windmills for the generation of clean energy? There have always been environmental wackos, but never had they had such an avid audience as the past administration, ready to cash in big-time and embrace them with open arms. Four trillion dollars are being earmarked for the advancement of the cap-and-trade bill. The Democratic House under its greedy and mindless head had given the nod for this fine arrangement.

Never mind the facts that come to light, that some of the scientists on whose research this science of manmade global warming was based are found to have falsified their data. The regulations that have been put in place continue to be enforced regardless of the fact that the whole thing was an unadulterated lie. And never mind the fact that the so-called dire effect of supposed global warming was light-years away. We were increasingly suffering the ravages of that current administration and its day-by-day actions to set the whole globe on fire by its handling of the Middle East and other Muslim places. (That was the real global warming—no, global burning—but more about that later.)

THE HEALTH-CARE BILL, THE CROWNING ACHIEVEMENT OF OUR LEADER

It was POTUS's burning desire to give every inhabitant of our land health insurance. This could have been achieved by taking a sum of taxpayer money and setting it aside just for that purpose to help those who needed help. Instead our wise leader and consultants had devised a (devilish) plan that started by taking away everybody's private insurance and making them get an insurance plan that the IRS oversaw. This plan would then pay for itself because the premiums the healthy paid would cover the cost for the sick.

One of the originators of this health-care plan, Jonathan Gruber, was later clearly heard saying that the only way this could be implemented was because Americans were stupid (The Hill, November tenth, 2014, by Elise Viebeck.) Its intention was to subjugate us all as part of POTUS's agenda coming straight from the bible by Saul Alinsky, *Rules for Radicals*.

But be that as it may, the health-care bill was looming large on the horizon next, and the leader said that not passing it was not an option. No sane person wanted this bill, which would truly take away our freedom and our very lives in fact. The thought of it made me cringe and shudder. A bureaucrat would be placed between a patient and his or her doctor to decide whether the patient was productive enough for the greater good of society to get a procedure done, have a surgery allowed, or have a medicine prescribed. The former Republican candidate for vice president had accurately described this proposal during her candidacy, stating, there will be death panels established which can pass judgement on our destiny.

But it was literally shoved down our throats and became law by she-nanigans and crookedness in the middle of the night with bribery and blackmail thrown in. The law was again thousands of pages long, and Congresswoman Nancy Pelosi, the majority leader, sweetly declared that it should be passed first then read, an idea that only someone with derangement in the brain could advance, and only deranged minds could agree to vote for. But it passed, and it was immediately hailed as the shining achievement of our leader. (Not one single Republican voted for that bill!)

Since the ratification of this bill by Congress had been hard work for our leader—and just in case Congress was less than forthcoming next time—some forty czars were put in place, each one a devoted progressive, to help the leader govern and thus circumvent Congress, which along with our Constitution became more and more irrelevant.

Some of what went on day by day was enough to send one into permanent dejection. A pamphlet was distributed to veterans, those who gave their all for us. It was a death book that gently suggested suicide to those who were in wheelchairs, in nursing homes, or simply in a blue mood because of what they saw in the hell of war. (The pamphlet was called "Your Life: Your Choices", a ten-year old directive published by the VA, which had been discarded by President Bush. Obama revived it in 2009 with the implied message: hurry up and die.) Those items alone—the death panels and the death book—would help defray the $3 trillion to $4 trillion the enforcement of the health-care law would require. Most of the money, though, would come from the young, who had to enroll and pay for health care whether they wanted to or not, or they would have to pay a stiff fine. There were rumors circulated by those few legislators who read some of the law, that young men's health-care plans included payment for pregnancy whether they were pregnant or not. They also had to pay for prevention-of-pregnancy devices and pills whether they used them or not. One never knows. After all it was truly an all-encompassing, compassionate health-care plan, according to POTUS.

A WELL-DESERVED VACATION

It was time for a vacation for the hardworking leader, and the topic of the media had switched. The health-care law had aroused some of the average folks from their deep sleep, and they went to town meetings to express their concern, peacefully but definitively. The Tea Party was formed, consisting of groups of ordinary citizens who had never been involved in protests before but who were very disturbed at what they saw happening. To distract them, the attorney general took it upon himself to question CIA operatives to see if the previous administration had broken any laws after 9/11 while it kept us safe. Waterboarding, (a method of extracting information by holding a person's head under water for some time, until they absolutely needed to breathe) became a big topic and was discussed at length. It was thought to be cruel and had to be forbidden, even though it had only been done to three of the main terrorist prisoners and had given us important information. In addition, some of our own soldiers were routinely waterboarded when training for special ops.

MORE GOVERNING

The Anointed One then came back refreshed from his vacation, and the abominations continued. Indoctrination of schoolchildren was the next agenda. While kindergarteners were taught songs about the greatness of our supreme leader, the National Endowment for the Arts, under Obama's directive, was supporting artists who brought forth works of art with helpful themes such as how wonderful the health-care law was and the infinite economic benefit of turning to green energy. Furthermore, the First Lady told us what we should eat and drink. And, yes, the wackos prescribed what kind of toilet paper was OK to use. Eventually the First Lady arranged for lunches to be given to schoolchildren that were healthy for them, taking away stuff that they liked to eat. The result of this maneuver was that many of the kids threw their lunches, which we taxpayers paid for, in the garbage, and they snacked on the stuff sneaked in from home.

Next, a huge nest of corruption came to light through the courageous work of some young investigative reporters, which pervaded a non-profit organization (ACORN) with many arms and branches, all heavily endowed by taxpayer moneys and stimulus funds. For example, ACORN received four hundred and forty-six billion taxpayer dollars in the state of Illinois. ACORN had been helpful in many ways regarding the election and community organizing, a specialty of Obama. In fact, he was instrumental in teaching the group its fundamentals. ACORN also was an important source of information for girls who had become pregnant through no fault of their own and needed abortions. There were specialists at ACORN who helped these young girls find what they wanted.

The mainstream media ignored the problem, except for some minor references. The exalted one, when asked about the large sums distributed to ACORN, typically claimed to know nothing about that. At least the Census Bureau, whose work ACORN was slated to do next, divested itself from the organization. The IRS and the stimulus distributors promised to cut further funding and to follow up with an investigation. (An investigation in this administration always meant to forget about the matter and move on. And ACORN continued to function unaltered except that each of the many branches was given some new, exotic name.)

In addition, the reporter who helped discover this fine, costly arrangement that our taxes financed and who reported on it to the conservative media, was found dead on the street one day, having perhaps suffered a heart attack. He was a man in his early forties and had just had drinks in a bar with a stranger. (Hmm, that sounds like a similar story I have heard, but I can't remember when or about whom. Was it about a justice? Maybe it will come to me later.)

IRAQ AND AFGHANISTAN

In the meantime, our troops were being called home from Iraq, the war that was so maligned. All the sacrifices of shed blood and maimed soldiers soon came to naught because the terrorists returned to their terrorist ways. The fragile government we established there was incapable of controlling the country. The war in Afghanistan, the one the commander in chief called the "good, important one," fared no better because he ignored the generals' calls for more soldiers and equipment; in fact during seven months at the front, the general in charge was able to speak only once with his commander in chief, who was busy jumping around the United States like a rabid kangaroo, making the rounds of all the TV stations—save the one that tells the truth—to sing the praises of his all-encompassing, compassionate health-care law, which no one with any brains wanted. (There were the polls to show it.)

THE CAP-AND-TRADE BILL

The next item on the agenda was the cap-and-trade bill, mentioned earlier, for green energy and to prevent global warming. The leader was on a roll, so there had to be a method to this madness to make it palatable to the common folks, and there was.

Very soon after the health-care bill passed, some curious accidents happened in short order; they could not have been timed any better if they had been planned. (Hmm, it makes you wonder.) Three coal mines incurred accidents in a short period of time. Some people died, but that did not seem to create the hoped-for result—no outrage ensued. So, lo and behold, a giant oil rig in the Gulf of Mexico exploded, and people died again. This time, the whole country was in uproar; all the radio stations were outraged at the evil oil companies. (What a superb coincidence!) The oil companies were demonized and made to pay an open-ended $20 billion to the federal government to be distributed for the damages done. The CEO of the oil company was raked over the coals (no pun intended), though he did what he could to stop the spill and clean up the damage in the water and on the coastlines.

The leader was in his glory, bounding from TV station to TV station, but all this time ignoring the pleas to help the affected states. In fact, he was dragging his feet even to inspect the damage firsthand or speak to the CEO overseeing damage control, claiming there was no point in speaking to him. Worse yet, he prevented all help offered from abroad and from our own country by bureaucratic means. He invoked some ancient law on the books (foreign vessels could not come close to our shores), and he claimed the help could damage our coastline. Instead, true to his agenda, he put a ban on drilling in the whole Gulf of Mexico, despite the fact that a federal judge overturned the ban. The result was that many people were out of work. The oil rigs departed for foreign lands. He finally had some photo ops on the Louisiana coast and promptly departed for another vacation.

(Now here is a puzzlement. Why did the former POTUS simply ignore that federal judge while now President Trump actually cannot keep his promise of stopping illegal immigration from seven ISIS countries and preventing the financing of sanctuary cities, because some lefty judges pronounce that he cannot? Strange!)

Chapter 3

THE STATE OF THE UNION

It became apparent to me that the leader who was elected without being vetted (except by some conservative commentators and a few conservative talk show hosts, who were not heard by the majority and ignored and denounced as freaks by others) seemed to be accomplished in not telling the truth. He had an agenda to bring the country down due to some deep-seated hatred for our nation and other hatreds he had internalized from his upbringing.

He had promised transparency in his administration, yet he passed laws in the dark of night with the Republican minority excluded from the deliberations. Didn't he promise no lobbyists? Yet lobbyists were everywhere. Didn't he promise the country was going to come together? We found ourselves divided in every way like never before: the rich against the poor, women against men, religion against religion, and Democrats against Republicans. Worst of all, he tried his best to pit race against race. He told us with a straight face that things were getting better when they were not and that the country's borders were more secure when they were not. He said he was responsible for the country producing more oil than ever before when the oil was not coming from federal lands but from private sources. Radicals had raised him. He had embraced radical ideas all his life and now surrounded himself with the most radical of his pals, who were conducting the business of governing the country.

As for the Democrats, they were nothing but robots, each one repeating what the other said. They talked in clichés and slogans; their eyes and faces reflected a certain quality of deadness. The ones in charge were visibly glassy eyed while pronouncing their lies. For example, they told us that the Arizona border had never been as safe as it was under the present leader, and they praised the economic benefits of the health-care law. It was what Ann Coulter called "demonic mob rule." It became unnecessary even to listen to what they had to say. I knew before they opened their mouths what was going to come out. They were as blind and allergic to facts as some people are genetically tone deaf to the modulation of sound. Facts did not matter if they did not coincide with their preconceived ideas, fed by the mainstream media. When I watched the news, which was increasingly fair and balanced on Fox News, I had to mute the comments made by the liberal contingent because my stomach could not take them anymore.

The thing that was most disturbing was the suspicion that there was a mastermind somewhere behind the administration who figured out every time what would most disturb ordinary citizens and conservatives. So, they came out every day with another regulation, edict, law, or order for doing business that would drive those people up a tree. For example, they sued the governor of Arizona for trying to enforce the law that the government should enforce to protect the border from illegals. Another order was not to build some pipeline to transport oil from our northern neighbor to Texas, which could bring in oil from a friendly country and create thousands of jobs. One mandated Catholic organizations to pay for contraception and abortion pills, which went against their beliefs and was deeply offensive to them. On many occasions God was eliminated from signs, prayers, the pledge of allegiance, and other places to show that the Judeo-Christian fundamental principles our country was founded on no longer applied.

Consider also the infringements put in place by the health-care law (almost every day we discovered a new horror in its many pages) and the thousands of regulations the EPA had to implement (despite the fact that manmade global warming is a ridiculous myth), each of which infringed on our freedom in a fundamental way and destroyed more of the economy, which was dismal to begin with. Take the fact that we were not allowed to drill in the Gulf of Mexico or Alaska, where our oil and a million jobs were waiting, unavailable. Instead, the government spent billions of dollars for green energy like the fiasco of Solyndra, which had received five hundred and thirty-five million dollars from the taxpayer kitty for producing solar energy, but went bankrupt. There were a number of other companies with similar results, having failed miserably to come to fruition. Take the takeover of the car industry, which resulted in the building of a tiny, combustible electric car costing a cool $40,000 nobody seemed to want. This one was one of my favorites because of the slogan that went with it: "Chevy runs deep"—a meaningful slogan that only a Harvard graduate could have approved. Then take the fast and furious debacle, in which American guns were sold to Mexican drug cartels in the purportedly innocent attempt to trace the drug pushers and growers, causing the murders of hundreds of Mexicans and an American border patrol agent. No one responsible was punished. Take the fact that we were now $16 trillion in debt. (The president said even after three and a half years of his administration that it was all Bush's fault).

There were many more instances, too many to mention. I concluded that the goal in reality was to bring the country into chaos and ruin. There were the so-called Occupy movements, young people sitting for days and nights in public places and creating filth, committing crimes, and spouting anti-Semitism. They were practicing to be personal mouthpieces for the regime. The leader and his minions praised them and looked up to them as the genuine counterpoint to the Tea Party, a group of orderly, mature citizens who just wanted their country and their freedom back.

Then I feared what secretive things were perhaps being built and established deep in Utah to monitor ordinary citizens.

(Fast forward: this latter all came to pass. We recently found out that everybody's phone calls and e-mails are being recorded and saved. Three hundred thirty million Americans are spied on. Thirty-five thousand Americans are actively monitored, which is supposed to require warrants, which were never obtained.)

Chapter 4

A SECOND TERM

Obama was very popular with members of his party, who loved all the freebies and attention they were getting and the fact that it was more financially profitable not to work. It has to be mentioned here that: 1) he had extended and increased unemployment insurance, 2) paid people to talk others into the use of food stamps, 3) given disability insurance freely to those who said they did not feel well and 4) donated free iPhones and the cost per months to welfare recipients, including illegals. But, there still was the matter of voting. He felt he needed some insurance. The president, with the help of the attorney general, put forth a mandate that allowed people to vote without photo identification in some states, which resulted in miraculous things. Dead Democrats were resurrected to vote. In addition, illegals voted to their hearts' content, and some voted numerous times in different places, getting paid by some generous special fund. One gentleman reported proudly that he had voted sixty-eight times. (I wonder if that's worth an entry in the *Guinness Book of World Records*.) Also, in 2012 they managed to avoid counting military votes because the Democrats in charge decided the votes did not arrive on time. (It was well known that most military personnel voted Republican.)

It was not all the Democrats' doing that Obama got reelected. Mitt Romney, the Republican candidate, badly flubbed the last debate for all to see by not touching on any of the grave sins that had been committed during POTUS's first term, giving him the election for the second term on a silver platter. The conservative Republicans and many citizens went into emotional despair, for they were fully awake by then and had given the Republican Party the House.

But no one complained openly, no one protested, no one broke into shops and public property, and no one staged riots, stopped traffic, or went on shooting rampages. No one asked to impeach POTUS despite the many illegal things he had done, despite having disregarded our Constitution, despite having disregarded Congress completely, and despite having gotten the goat of and produced ulcers in every conservative citizen alive. No one declared that the election had been stolen from them or counted the ways POTUS had cheated and connived to be illegally elected. Romney and Paul Ryan, the candidates for president and vice president respectively, simply went back to their former jobs and quietly licked their wounds. They did not voice again and again how they got cheated by POTUS to make them lose. They instead reflected on how they had failed and what they had done wrong. No one screamed, "Russia."

Chapter 5

WHAT DIFFERENCE DOES IT MAKE?

Enter a new character into our story: "What difference does it make?" said the most intelligent woman in the world in front of an inquiry when asked about the four Americans in Benghazi who had been sacrificed on the altar of the 2012 presidential election. She was the secretary of state of this administration, and she was enraged at having been put in the position of having to answer questions. What difference did it make when four Americans got killed, two Navy SEALs, a special service agent, and an ambassador, in light of the hundreds of Mexicans who were killed as well as an American border agent during the fast and furious debacle in which we supplied guns to drug lords? There was a Congressional inquiry into that mess, and they were going to get to the bottom of that—that is, the mess went away, and no one got punished. And what difference did it make if four good Americans were murdered in light of the thousands of Syrians getting killed with guns we had been supplying to the rebels in that mess? Those were just four Americans compared to thousands of other human beings, so what difference did it make? This was what this world had come to under this administration, and we were sitting still for this infinitely appalling turn of events. How did we get here? How did we get to this point of total callousness in four short years?

The statement was in answer to a specific inquiry by a committee of Congress as to why we were all lied to by the administration for weeks after the burning of the consulate in Libya. We were told that it was a spontaneous event due to a vile video someone had put on the Internet months before, a "despicable, vile" video that insulted the good Muslims to their core all over the place. We all knew it was an attack by Islamic extremists, but it occurred after the president had declared that the extremists had been defeated, and Osama bin Laden was dead.

Since this distracting event happened right in the midst of the 2012 campaign, the folks could not possibly be disturbed in any way by extraneous and contradictory information. So the whole thing was shoved under the rug and blamed on some reprehensible video that no one had seen. But what the heck? It saved the day for the president. (And the video producer was put in jail.) This lie was repeated for weeks, by the president, by the secretary of state, by the ambassador to the United Nations, and by the press secretary. How could we doubt it? And what difference did it make?

It turned out the story that Madam Secretary of State told was rather involved and would not go away. So many questions remained. Why was no help provided when there were seven hours during which we could have sent help? Who decided that no help should be provided? What was the president doing while the attack was going on? Who decided to cover up the truth with the story of the video that was put on the Internet months before and no one saw? Why did the secretary of state not send any reinforcements when that was asked repeatedly? She claimed she never even saw the note asking for the reinforcements. (And three years later, we found out that reinforcements were asked for six hundred times, but never provided.)

The Democrats, in their infinite wisdom, finally came up with an answer to all the questions: they pronounced it a witch hunt by Fox

News and the Republicans. After all, what difference did it make that four good Americans got killed at this point?

Although the fast and furious story, in which we sent guns to Mexico with disastrous results, somehow disappeared with no one held accountable, the story of Benghazi did not seem to go away.

NEW SCANDALS

And then some new floodgates opened: two more scandals appeared in short succession in a period of one week. There was a revelation, which had been festering but never had come out, that Tea Party groups, asking for tax-exempt status were targeted by the IRS not to be granted this exemption. Religious groups, other conservative groups, and pro-Israel groups got the same treatment. They were being asked innumerable personal questions and then not getting granted tax exempt status. People were asked who they prayed to, who their benefactors were, what they believed in, and what they ate for breakfast. It finally came out that the woman who was in charge of granting the tax-exempt status was promoted to Director of the Affordable Care Act Office of the IRS. She was going to oversee the implementation of the health-care law to make sure that every citizen (and noncitizen) had health insurance; those not in compliance would get punished with heavy fines. And before this promotion she got a healthy bonus ($70,000) for having done such an admirable job of the tax exemption business. In the interim it was made public that the IRS used credit cards to purchase wine, clothes, and pornography for their own use. Of course, they were going to get to the bottom of that—that is, it was declared that everything was OK after they looked into the targeting. One of the implementers, Lois Lerner, simply invoked the Fifth Amendment when asked whether targeting was going on. The matter disappeared, and she retired with a handsome pension.

While this lovely story appeared, some whistleblowers revealed that a bunch of Republican reporters had been followed on the Internet and by phone bugging as to who they communicated with, who they consorted with, and what they were going to print or say. This was so toxically illegal, it defied the imagination.

The Attorney General of the United States swore to Congress under oath that he would never have asked for or done such a thing. He was aghast and could not imagine anyone would do this! Yet several days later, it was discovered that he himself had actually signed off on this fine arrangement for the chief correspondent of Fox News, that pesky truth-telling channel. Even the reporter's parents were being monitored and harassed.

But this was a mere bagatelle for the attorney general. This same attorney general had disregarded the new Black Panther intimidation of white folks voting in Philadelphia during the 2008 election and had handled the fast and furious matter with the outcome that no one got punished. He was a pro. Many people asked for his resignation, but he remained steadfast in his position, saying he had some more very important things to do before leaving the administration.

We are living in a police state, that is for sure. Our lives are being monitored and watched, and our freedoms have surely disappeared.

A new scandal followed the others in short order: namely, a young gentleman from the National Security Agency (NSA) came forward to tell us that all our telephone calls and Internet communications were monitored by the administration to be accumulated in an immense new facility built deep in Utah. (See chapter 3.) When asked about this disaster of eroding the privacy of every citizen, members of the NSA proclaimed that the matter was done for our own protection, and no one's phone calls or e-mail were listened to or read.

After the IRS targeted Tea Party members and religious groups for the political gain of the Democrats, who with any gray matter in his or her head would believe this new fabrication of no listening and no peeking? The gentleman who informed us of this matter was called a traitor by the administration and was pursued to be put in prison forthwith. The conservatives called him a hero for letting us know what we were in for. Strangely enough, he asked for and got asylum in Russia, though he would have liked to go to somewhere in South America. He promised to reveal more goodies about the administration as time went on and, when appropriate, give the explanations of various lies that we were saddled with.

RUSSIA TO THE RESCUE

When all these scandals—plus the disregard of the Constitution and law and order—accumulated to a critical mass so that the poll numbers of the commander in chief were going south, he came up with the brilliant idea of attacking Syria, which had been killing its citizens by the thousands since the civil war began. POTUS told us that now was the time to attack Syria because they had resorted to using chemical weapons, and he could not tolerate that. It was baffling that killing thousands by shooting them with guns (some provided by us) seemed to be tolerable, but now that the scandals were filling some of the news, it was time to change the subject.

The American citizens did not want any part of attacking Syria, but he insisted, telling us first that he had the executive power to do it. When some members of Congress complained that starting a war was not constitutional without its approval, the president declared that he would consult them, but if they did not agree, he would attack Syria anyway. He had announced about a year before that if chemical weapons were moved or used, that would indicate a red line beyond which he would change his calculus and would have to attack. (What calculus had to do with it, I do not know. But then, that subject always was a mystery to me.)

This whole back-and-forth filled the newspapers and the news on the radio and TV. The citizens were distracted, and the aforementioned scandals were all forgotten. In between the president playing golf and going for a quick trip to Europe to attend a summit meeting, the Brits told him that they would not go to war with Syria for him. France vacillated, saying they would only help in a minor way. POTUS had painted himself in a corner. Our citizens mostly wanted no part of this idea, nor did Congress, even though he met the Republicans at lunches and dinners, a first for this president (after he had ignored them for the past four years), to persuade them of the humanitarian necessity to attack. While this was happening, the murder of Syrians never stopped, nor did other killings all over the Middle East, and the four Americans in Libya were left to be murdered, being an inconvenient distraction at the time due to the upcoming election.

Guess who came to the rescue? Russian president Vladimir Putin announced that he would persuade Syrian president Bashar al-Assad to give up the toxic weapons to an international committee. POTUS postponed the vote by Congress, which he knew would never pass. There came the Russians to the rescue. Promptly, the Democrats said POTUS had won a big victory with his threats of going to war, and now it would all be resolved diplomatically. What a coup!

POTUS was delighted with this outcome and felt that he, with his threats to go to war, had put one over on the Russians. The whole thing would be resolved. What a clever maneuver on his part. He basked in the effect he had had and appointed John Kerry to be the implementer of the good tidings after Mrs. "What Difference Does It Make?" resigned her post as secretary of state to gather the millions needed for her campaign in 2016. John Kerry was to make sure that the international community was directed to follow our lead in assuring peace in Syria and also to deter Iran from its continuing efforts to produce atomic weapons (for now).

It was a fun time for the Anointed One, gloating over his accomplishments in foreign policy. By all means he would give the Iranians, who had elected a new and rather friendly, smooth-talking president, all they wanted in relaxing the boycott that had been put in place and had been effective in delaying the bomb project, so they could feed their population again; in return, they would allow the UN to see a couple of their ten thousand centrifuges, busy enriching uranium for their atomic bombs. The French were aghast at this idea and said they wanted no part of this deal. Israel said this was a very bad deal. The Saudis and Jordanians also voiced their disapproval. POTUS continued to push forward, but other troubles occupied him at that moment.

Chapter 6

MORE GOVERNING: THE HEALTH-CARE LAW, PHASE TWO

Meanwhile the health-care law had given a few headaches to its head honcho, who tried to raise money for it by approaching various insurance companies, Hollywood celebrities, and others to close the gap of billions of dollars required for its implementation. In addition, the administration tried various means to interest young folks, schools, and others to bring forth propaganda for this crowning achievement of the president. He himself ran around the country in between various vacations to praise the all-encompassing, passionate law with passionate words, saying even that it was a civil right for each and every one of us to have health insurance. He tried to engage a famous TV personality, Oprah Winfrey, to approach her humongous audience with glowing words of the wonderful health-care law. Since the money for the law was still not available despite the machinations put forth, he wisely postponed its implementation for some time, assuring various unions, cronies, and Congress that they would be exempt from this law. What generosity on the one side and what total unfairness to the American people! (Was this colossal chutzpah even believable or digestible?)

But there is much more to come. So, let us fast forward.

THE HEALTH-CARE LAW, PHASE THREE

October 1, 2013, rolled around, the date the health-care law was to be implemented, but the promised easy way to get to the insurance market, by going on the Internet and simply enrolling, did not work.

First Lady Michelle Obama had a close friend from her days in Princeton with whom she had been very in tune. (At that time they both belonged to a group not too friendly to the Israelis but enthralled with the PLO). This friend and her husband were living in Canada now and had started a company devoted to fixing websites, especially in the field of health-care enrollments. Their expertise must have been kind of rusty. Even though the administration had given them six million cool dollars from the taxpayers' kitty to implement the site for easy access from October 1 to November 20, the site only worked minimally and occasionally. In fact, six people were able to look at the site on October 1, and soon after, only a trickling of people could follow suit. Since the law was taking effect nonetheless, five million insured people, happy with their private health insurance, lost it as mandated by the all-encompassing, compassionate health-care law from POTUS. These people were up in arms, left without health insurance and with no way to enroll in the new one. This mess finally hit home; it affected both liberals and the horrible conservatives. The trouble was that the Democratic legislators in Republican states got really upset at this problem and started to voice their opinions; they tried to distance themselves from POTUS's crowning achievement.

Soon the administration had to do something. POTUS went on the air to state he had known nothing about the defective Internet site, but he would soon get to the bottom of it and fix it. Then it came out that the administration had been aware of all this since 2010, and so he went on the air and declared it was indirectly his fault and apologized for it. Congresswoman Pelosi said at the very same time that POTUS had done nothing wrong. Oprah Winfrey announced on TV that the hullabaloo was really all a racist thing. The implementer in chief for the health-care law claimed that it was all Fox News's fault. The situation finally resolved itself, as expected, when POTUS went on the air once more to affirm it really all was the Republicans' fault, although not one single solitary Republican had voted for this law.

THE HEALTH-CARE LAW, PHASE FOUR

By the end of November, the Internet site was sort of fixed, but a new problem arose in the meantime. Some of the people applying for health insurance on this site discovered that complete strangers were privy to their most intimate information, and it was being used nefariously. It turned out that the health insurance Internet site was not secure in any way, shape, or form. Hackers were busy hacking. Between the data gathering that was going to Utah (for our safety) and the data obtained from people enrolling in health insurance, personal privacy was a thing of the past for every citizen. (Friends knew who had venereal diseases, and the government knew how they had gotten it.)

In addition, it turned out that, for the average person who had lost his or her insurance, health insurance through the Obamacare exchanges was much more expensive. Copays were massive compared to the ones they used to pay. As if that were not enough, it seemed that the people who were applying were mainly the older and sick population. This was not so good for the financing of the health-care law because it was the younger, healthy people who were supposed to pay their premiums to subsidize the cost for the elderly, sick population, as mentioned before. That had been the scheme of the leader and his minions all along. So much for the all-encompassing, compassionate health-care law.

By the end of the year, two million people had insured themselves, according to the administration, and this was bandied about as a major victory. (Just to be precise, the population of the United States is 330 million, give or take a few.)

No one was told, however, if these two million had paid up. Rumors roamed around that the insurance companies involved were not quite sure if they had obtained the data correctly or were aware of persons really being insured when it came to seeing a doctor in the future. There seemed to be no visible reckoning.

The crowning glory for the health-care law was that for POTUS to have said twenty-nine times that "you could keep your health care if you liked your health care, and you could keep your doctor if you liked your doctor" and everyone would save a goodly amount of money, at least $2,500 a year per family, he earned himself the Liar of the Year Award at the end of 2013 from PolitiFact. (That, in fact, was his one and only accomplishment that could be pointed to as being honestly true and honestly earned in the five years of his administration up to that point.)

The next outrage that came out in the newspapers was that it would be up to Kathleen Sibelius (the Secretary of Health and Human Services) to tell your doctor, the one you paid for with your new health insurance, what kind of treatment to give and procedure to do. Was she ever anywhere near a medical school? Had she even walked into one or had private tutoring in medicine? It eventually came out that the IRS, which was partly responsible to administer Obamacare, had lost $67 million from its Obamacare fund. The whole thing was so absurd and so outrageous. We were in what I could call, for lack of another expression, a cyclone of wicked absurdities because of how many there were and how fast they were coming at us.

OBAMACARE, PHASE FIVE

Things did not get better in 2014. The health-care law had to be altered thirty-nine times by POTUS because the money was not there, the people complained bitterly when taken off the health insurance they liked, the website was still tenuous, and Congress complained that POTUS changed the law all by himself when it was the job of Congress to do that as ensured by the Constitution. (Caring about the Constitution was about the last thing this supposed scholar of that document was interested in. Subjugating people was the thing to do, and the number one way to do it, is to take over their healthcare, according to the principles enunciated by Alinsky.)

Chapter 7

STATE OF THE UNION, PHASE TWO

My patience was fast coming to an end, my outrage had come to an explosive point, and my fury was getting the better of me. We could make another list of how this country was faring and going downhill more every day.

There was for instance a mandate given to the Little Sisters of the Poor, a Catholic order of nuns who had taken care of dying poor people for the past 165 years so in their last moments, they were not left all to themselves with no one there to help them through. The anointed leader of our country was now threatening these nuns with a stiff fine, which would put them out of business, if they didn't pay for the health care of their employees. They, nevertheless, refused to pay for this health care, as it included abortion, sterilization, and contraception, because these were deeply offensive to their religious beliefs. Since they insisted on not paying for these services and medications, the attorney general proceeded to sue the nuns—truly a saintly job, one of the things he was anxious to do when he said he needed to accomplish still more for this administration. (See chapter 5.)

The economy limped along: approximately fifty million people were on food stamps with the active encouragement of paid volunteers to bring more on board.

A piece of legislation was being discussed that would make illegal citizens vote for the Democrats and get paid for it, so the Democrats would remain in office forever.

The next thing on the agenda was the appointment of a civil rights judge to the judicial department. The man the Anointed One, together with his attorney general, picked was a lawyer who had volunteered to commute the sentence of a cop killer after thirty years of his being on death row. He had been duly convicted and sentenced to death, having shot a cop four times in cold blood. The sentence was then commuted to life imprisonment. The gentleman who commuted this sentence was now the number one pick to oversee our civil rights.

GLOBAL WARMING, PHASE TWO

In further reassurance to the fact of global warming (if it were not sad, it would be very comical), a group of scientists from various parts of the world took a trip in a ship to a corner of the sea near Antarctica to accurately measure how much the ice was melting there, promising to do it to the hundredth of a milliliter. Lo and behold, the ship got near Antarctica and promptly got very much frozen in there because the ice was so thick; the ship could not budge. After some ten days of trying to maneuver, the ship was declared officially stuck. A helicopter was ordered to take the scientists out in groups of a few at a time. The professors were taken onto another ship to bring them back home. This ship also got stuck in the thick ice. The rescue helicopter was now frozen, too. But—and this is the best part of the story—after hearing about all this for several days, a progressive super scientist par excellence declared to all who would listen that the whole thing was indeed due to global warming and was to be expected. (You sure can't make this stuff up, as Hannity often says in desperation. It has a beauty of its own.)

Chapter 8

THE STATE OF THE WORLD

In this easily won second term of the Anointed One, so many terrible things were happening due to the stratagems of the administration that it would be hard to keep it all in chronological order.

1) The war between the citizens of Syria and the people in power continued unabated with hundreds of thousands of people dead.

2) Iran continued to prepare atomic weapons and missiles to carry them far away while POTUS negotiated and gave them the money that had been withheld effectively before, because Iran promised to let a few UN people in to observe a couple of their ten thousand centrifuges; however, the Iranian ruler stipulated they had to give twenty-four days' notice. While he was negotiating, there were still four American prisoners in Iran. Kerry, the negotiator, never mentioned them until the deal was made and then sent a plane filled with $400 million in cash to get three of the prisoners freed. The fourth was not heard from again. In addition, we found out that Iran was free to build nuclear weapons after fifteen years under this great deal POTUS signed off on.

3) The administration had been financially helping the Arab Brotherhood, a group in Egypt that was fanatical in its views, wanted to create a caliphate, and followed Sharia law. The Egyptians rebelled against the brotherhood on its way to implement Sharia law and managed to fight them successfully, much to the chagrin of our leader. (I wonder what that revealed about him. Nobody ever explained the meaning of his affinity for the Muslim Brotherhood.)

4) After POTUS called our troops home from Iraq, which he termed the evil war, though we had made progress there after President Bush allowed more soldiers to fight, Iraq became a vacuum attracting the worst of the worst. It was being invaded by a terrorist group even more vicious than Al-Qaeda and Hamas. They called themselves ISIS, the Islamic State of Iraq, but POTUS liked to call them ISIL, the Islamic State of the Levant (that is, all the Middle East, including Israel).

There would have been plenty of time to prevent this group's progress using drones and attacking them by air in the region as they invaded city upon city by foot in open territory, but POTUS refused to do anything. ISIS was well on its way to eventually establishing a caliphate from Iraq to Turkey, Syria, and other areas of Africa.

The group grew by leaps and bounds. They took advantage of the oil that was left for immense amounts of money and the weapons that they found, left by American troops. They were ruthless against the inhabitants of the region and encouraged new members to join them with the money they had at their disposal, not only from the oil, but also from taking people hostage and demanding huge amounts of money for their return.

They killed by cutting off people's heads, including children and babies, whose heads they impaled on fences. They burned people alive in cages and maimed and raped their way forward. POTUS finally declared that it was global warming that made them do this, and others of the Democratic persuasion said that they just needed jobs, education, and love.

5) Hamas attacked Israel again and again. After launching thousands of rockets into cities and populated areas to kill as many Israelis as they could, they built underground tunnels going from Gaza into Israel with the money the United States gave them to build hospitals and homes. They infiltrated Israel, killed citizens, and captured others. Three Israeli teenagers were captured at a bus stop near their school. After people spent months looking for them, they were found dead and buried in shallow graves. This dastardly deed finally got the Israelis, who had been living for years with constant rocket barrages, to invade Gaza to try to stop the murdering of their citizens. They did this in the most humane way possible, by warning the citizens of Gaza with leaflets strewn from the air and telephone calls and text messages to leave the areas they intended to bomb. They even dropped fake bombs to scare the civilians away before each launch of the real ones. But Hamas told these same people to stay where they were and not to heed the Israeli warnings. Thus, hundreds of Palestinians were killed. This was exactly what Hamas had wanted to accomplish, to make the Israelis look bad in front of the world when they were just trying finally to defend themselves.

And this propaganda worked. Anti-Semitism in Europe and the United States grew greatly with demonstrations against Jews and the killing of Jews in France, Belgium, the Netherlands, and other places. Jewish students in various colleges here, including the Ivy League schools, were harassed and declared to favor apartheid and land stealing when it was the Palestinians who caused havoc in Israel. In hopes of gaining peace, the Israelis had given them from their land—tiny compared to the immense Arab nations—a flourishing, beautiful area replete with vegetation brought forth from barren soil, Gaza. They soon destroyed the area and used it to launch rockets into Israel instead.

6) Putin invaded Crimea and annexed it and more of the land around it to Russia. It became a war zone. Airplanes were shot out of the air from that area, including one passenger plane with 296 people on board. It took a long time to gather the corpses and bring them home. The majority of the passengers were from the Netherlands, but there were also people from other parts of the world, including some Americans. The recovery was hampered for weeks because the locals did not allow access and looted the cargo. POTUS stood by during all these happenings. He did nothing and said nothing.

7) POTUS advertised in Central America for children to come to our land. The result was an invasion by alien children and women by the thousands coming from Central America to get amnesty. They brought with them diseases, lice, and skin disorders, which were promptly passed on to the border patrol agents and their families. (There was one American in prison in Mexico for making a mistake when traveling and taking a wrong turn, which landed him in that country, but POTUS did not say a word or move a finger to get him home.)

8) He then declared amnesty to be a civil right and by executive order decreed that those illegals who had been in this country for five years and committed no criminal act should register so they would not be deported, could get work permits, and could obtain driver's licenses, which would allow them to vote and get tax refunds. This was happening while 80 percent of the citizens wished to have no part of this amnesty and while some fifty

million citizens had no jobs. He had the gall to make some who had jobs train the illegals who then were allowed to take over the Americans' jobs.

9) In the meantime, the IRS checked on churches to make sure there was no political preaching. But no one was allowed into mosques, where preaching was often going on concerning killing Christians, Jews, Americans, and Muslim nonbelievers.

10) Finally, POTUS ensured that our defense department became so poor that we could not even defend ourselves. The military was too weak to defend our own soil. They had antiquated weapons, ships, and airplanes. Their numbers were drastically reduced, and their weapons did not function.

I declared in 2010 that POTUS wanted to create chaos and ruin in our beautiful country. Six years into his administration, we were way past this prediction. In fact, the whole globe was at a point of destruction. A crazed few people in Iran were at the helm of atomic bombs and the long-range missiles to launch them with, declaring clearly that Israel, the little Satan, had to be wiped off the face of the earth. And then the United States, the big Satan, had to be destroyed next.

ISIS continued to advance into Iraq with the help of Syria and Iran.

The next interim move toward our ruin was to bring the Ebola virus into this country from Africa by allowing two infected Americans back home before they were cured and by inviting a large group of so-called scientists to come from Africa to the United States for a meeting to discuss this disease, which was running rampant in Africa, killing thousands. In addition, POTUS sent three thousand soldiers to the infected region to help with curing the Ebola patients. What the result would be for our soldiers and country should have been thought about and feared. What an evil brainstorm this was to expose our young men, who had no training in or medical knowledge for such a job they never volunteered for. POTUS, with his wide knowledge of medicine, told us that the risk of an outbreak in our country was very low. No sooner was this said than a man came here from Africa and died of the disease. A nurse tending to him got infected, too.

Due to our medical acumen and some good luck, a doctor who had been tending to the sick over in Africa came home and was cured. A nurse from that same place, receiving some serum from the cured doctor, got well, too. A third person was not so lucky and died from the disease.

Truthfully the thing that I and others feared most was an epidemic like the one in Africa. Thankfully, this did not occur because of our country's first-class medical knowledge and despite POTUS's best efforts.

Chapter 9

TRUE GLOBAL WARMING

Things were heating up everywhere. ISIS made steady progress, taking over Iraq and going on a rampage, murdering thousands. They established their headquarters in Syria. They murdered Christians and Muslim minorities, those who were not willing to be extremists. But our eminent leader called them a sideshow, a JV team; he would manage them, but he did nothing when they were still vulnerable. When they became strong, numerous, and prosperous, he wanted to fight them—but not by boots on the ground. He used drones to kill a few when it was much too late. He was waiting to build a coalition to help him.

POTUS declared that ISIL was not Islamic and forbade the use of the phrase *Islamic terrorism* by our citizens. He solemnly pronounced that we would never be at war with Islam. And our new attorney general declared that terrorism would be defeated with love.

To show its true intents, ISIS proceeded to behead two reporters, one an American who had spent time aiding the natives and the other British. They showed the beheadings clearly on the Internet. Our citizens were appalled by this and clamored for someone to do something about them. So POTUS reluctantly bombed some sites in Iraq and in Syria, announcing that he had been able to form a coalition with some

Arab states for this endeavor. But ISIS continued to advance undeterred, and the bombings accomplished nothing except killing some civilians.

The fight between the Israelis and Hamas in Gaza continued, while cease-fires were declared on and off because Hamas kept up sending missiles into Israel, cease-fire or not. When a cease-fire finally held, Israel was unsure how many underground tunnels were left viable.

On vacation in Martha's Vineyard, our compassionate Anointed One finally found someone he could really do something for; he announced to Israel that he would no longer send them the wherewithal to defend themselves so they would stop fighting and killing civilians. But he was not finished with Israel. The UN, with his approval, resolved that Israel had no business building homes for Jews in Judea, Samaria, and eastern Jerusalem. So, the UN decided to end these constructions, and POTUS, as a farewell gesture, allowed this verdict to stand by not vetoing it, as previous presidents had invariably done. It then was resolved that Israel had no right to Jerusalem or the lands they had annexed in the 1967 war; they had to observe the previous borders, which were indefensible from the Arabs.

No matter—I heard with my own ears POTUS declaring that our country and the globe had never been as peaceful as they were now, not for a long time. What planet was the man living on?

MORE GOVERNING

Most people were now getting part-time jobs because the health-care law was too expensive for businesses to hire full-time employees who required health insurance. Fifty million people were still on food stamps, and ninety-two million people were out of work, but POTUS announced that the economy was booming.

A repeating mantra was that gun control should be imposed, but he was never bothered by the most gun-controlled city of Chicago, where young African Americans were killing one another daily.

By executive order, he declared that we would have regular relations and trade with Cuba from now on and established an ambassadorship there.

He was anxious to close Guantanamo Bay, a prison holding the most egregious of terrorists who wanted to kill us all. He let some out time after time and sent them back to the Middle East, where they were honored and welcomed to go back to work at war against us.

He declared war on carbon. He actually promised early on in his tenure to bankrupt the coal industry. The Keystone Pipeline, which for at least seven years had been studied and declared safe for the environment, was approved by the Republican Congress to be build. But he vetoed the bill, and thousands of jobs were lost again to the American people just for the hell of it. He declared that he had not had enough time to study its effects on the environment, that it would benefit Canada more than America, and only a few hundred jobs would be gained—not enough even to count.

RESEARCH ACCORDING TO THIS REGIME

Funding for the great National Institutes of Health was drastically cut. While researchers were now studying the Ebola virus, a very risky undertaking, the following research had been funded amply by this administration: the study of the sex lives of flies, a very serious scientific problem that needed to be solved with great speed; the elucidation of duck genitalia (Nobel Prize work); the behavior of drunk monkeys; and the strange occurrence of obesity in homosexual women. I am not quite sure why men were being discriminated against in this research proposal. They really should have protested and sued in line with the times we were in—but so be it.

Allowing two hundred thousand Muslims into the country who were supposedly running from ISIS (who really knew how many of them were mixed in with those refugees) and placing them quietly into red states in the middle of the night to create diversity was another scheme to create Democratic Party voters where those were in the minority. He later even went further. The new citizens would no longer have to swear allegiance to our laws and would not have to take up arms to defend our country.

Chapter 10

TERRORISM BY LONE WOLVES

Within a few years, ISIS had such an impact on young, vulnerable, disenfranchised, and desensitized young people (with the impact of TV and movies helping—Hollywood at its best) that many answered the call of jihad and became an army of lone wolves, often homegrown, having made contact on the Internet or by travel to the ISIS home bases. Some worked in small groups; some were all alone.

On November 28, 2008, ten Pakistani terrorists attacked in Mumbai, India, resulting in one hundred sixty-six deaths in two hotels and a Jewish center. This atrocity was executed by a forerunner of ISIS, another terrorist group.

On November 5, 2009, thirteen soldiers, including a pregnant woman, were shot and killed. Thirty were injured in Fort Hood, Texas, by Army Major Nidal Hasan, a Muslim psychiatrist, no less, who yelled "Allahu Akbar" while he committed this dastardly act. He was an American whom his superiors had been warned about by some of his coworkers; he seemed to have strange ideas. But no one heeded the warnings. There was no defense at the base because, believe it or not, the military personnel on the military bases were not allowed to have arms (compliments of POTUS).

On March 19, 2012, in Toulouse and Montauban, France, three French paratroopers and four Jewish people in a Hebrew school were killed (a teacher and three students.)

On November 13, 2015, in Paris, one hundred twenty-eight people were killed and hundreds injured by gunmen and suicide bombers in a concert hall, some restaurants, and a stadium.

On July 14, 2016, Bastille Day, in Nice, France, on the famous Avenue Des Anglais, a truck rushed into the crowd, killing eighty-four people and injuring fifty.

On July 7, 2015, five marines were killed in a military recruitment center at a mall in Chattanooga, Tennessee, by a Muslim who was an American citizen and had gone to Jordan to get jihadized. They were unable to defend themselves because there, too, they were forbidden to have arms. It took five days for the flag to be lowered at the White House.

On June, 12, 2016, forty-nine people were killed and fifty-three injured at a club in Orlando, Florida, by an American shooter who pledged allegiance to ISIS. The perpetrator's parents had come from Afghanistan and raised him as a Muslim.

On April 15, 2013, during the Boston Marathon, two jihadist brothers made bombs out of pressure cookers, which massacred three and wounded hundreds of young innocents. The Russian embassy had warned that one of the brothers had traveled back and forth to be trained by ISIS.

On December 2, 2015, fourteen people were killed and twenty-two seriously injured by a mass shooting and attempted bombing in San Bernardino, California, by a jihadist American, born in Pakistan, helped by his bride, who had recently come from Saudi Arabia and was also born in Pakistan. Neighbors had observed bombs and other paraphernalia in their home but said nothing because the word was out since the beginning of POTUS's reign that it was forbidden to talk about Muslims in terms of being terrorists. You had to be politically correct at all times even if you saw potential mayhem and murder.

Chapter 11

THE WAR ON THE POLICE, OR THE HANDLING OF THE POLICE DURING OBAMA'S REIGN

On July 7, 2016, a man hidden in a garage stooped down and assassinated five Dallas police officers and wounded seven others. Two days before this killing, two black men were killed in separate events, one in Louisiana and one in Minnesota, while not obeying police commands to give themselves up. According to the perpetrator, he killed the officers in Dallas because he was upset about white policemen killing blacks. The police had actually been in that area to protect a so-called peaceful demonstration for the two men killed. (The question is why there is this focus on whites killing blacks when it should be emphasized instead that police need to be obeyed.)

The real reason these people were killed, whether it was in Ferguson, Baltimore (see below), or anyplace else is they simply did not obey the law.

Why don't those accusing the police of racism see that we have a black president, a black attorney general, and many black people in other high-level governmental positions? Many Police chiefs in fact, are black. And yet they say blacks are being persecuted. In Chicago, many young black men kill one another over gang-related matters and drug wars, and no one speaks about it. Five hundred black youths were killed in

Chicago between January and June of 2016, with many more injured. This seems to be OK. It is mind-boggling. Recently, Jesse Jackson and the Reverend Al Sharpton, close confidants and advisers to POTUS, said the many shootings in Chicago of young men killing each other, was the fault of the Tea Party.

The statistics say there are three or four more shootings by black police officers than there are by white officers. The latter always hesitate because of political correctness and thus sometimes get killed themselves. (What's up with that—as the kids say?)

How did this war on the police start? Let us try to find the source.

Early on in POTUS's term in office, an officer stopped to ask an African American gentleman what he was doing. He had been in front of his house for some time, fiddling in his pocket to find his key and then, when he couldn't find the key, tried to break the lock. Though the neighborhood in Cambridge, Massachusetts, was predominantly white, it was an innocent enough question, to ask anybody, trying to break a lock! POTUS immediately—without waiting for an investigation—went on the air to say that the police had acted stupidly. This started a whole harangue, occupied the media, and became ingrained in the minds of sensitive youth. After all, it came from the president himself, and he made it a big point of contention.

Later in his term, an African American youth was shot in Sanford, Florida, after he hassled a Hispanic youth who was a neighborhood watchman. The Hispanic tried to defend himself, but the young man, husky and heavy, landed on his body and proceeded to knock his head against the concrete of the sidewalk repeatedly. Fearing for his life, the Hispanic youth unfortunately saw no way out, but to shoot the assailer. This brought about a big to-do. POTUS got involved immediately, and though it was a fight between members of two minorities, the fact that a black kid got killed was enough to lead POTUS—without an investigation—to get into it and inspire the black community to chalk it up to racism.

In Ferguson, Missouri, a black youth who had just harassed a worker in a liquor store, intending to rob it, accosted a police officer who had told him to stop walking in the middle of the street and wanted to arrest him. The youth came over threateningly and tried to grab his handgun. Then the policeman shot him in defense. For days after that, many youths rioted, looted, and destroyed the area's businesses. POTUS, without waiting for an investigation, condemned the shooting of an unarmed African American youth. The investigation showed that the police officer was well within his rights, as the youth had menaced him. In addition, a lie was put forward that the youth had been shot in the back while holding up his arms, seeming to surrender peacefully. This lie grew legs, and the movement talked about below took it as part of their slogan, holding up their arms while chanting. Of course, rioting and looting of the businesses in the area followed.

In Baltimore, Maryland, rioting for weeks resulted from a police incident in which a black youth was arrested for carrying an illegal switchblade. While he was transported to the police station, he got injured and later that week died from his injuries. Without waiting for an investigation, youths started rioting, and POTUS involved himself. Later the police officer was found innocent of the death. Baltimore was looted, and more businesses were destroyed than in Ferguson. Many never recovered.

All these incidents resulted in a group getting together and founding a movement, calling themselves Black Lives Matter, chanting, "What do we want? We want dead cops. When do we want them? We want them now." POTUS and the Democratic candidate for 2016 legitimized this group. They invited the group into the Democratic Convention, while five cops were killed in Dallas, Texas, and others were killed in many other locations. It was the thing to do—to shoot cops, and still is. Last week, a beautiful young mother of three was shot and killed, sitting in her police car with her partner, in New York City.

Not a word was heard from the last administration against these killings, nor was it ever mentioned that an average of thirty-two black youths are killed by other black youths per week in Chicago, the home city of POTUS with his best confidant and former chief of staff as a mayor. This did not fit into the agenda of cops killing black youths, and so it was not bothered with. It was not in the media; they were busy distributing the lies that were daily fillers for weeks.

During the 2012 election cycle, POTUS let out a secret that was actually a major factor in his character. Since some of the Democrats running for congress in Republican states did not want him to campaign with them, he said loud and clear that he was sorry they did not because campaigning was his favorite thing to do. (Now that was true, for anything else, like running the country, with its many facets that had nothing to do with the basic agenda he was pursuing of ruining it, was surely a drag.)

Just to reiterate, there were terrorist attacks in Brussels, Paris, Toulouse, Nice, Fort Hood, Boston, San Bernardino, and Orlando, but POTUS told us with a straight face that during his eight years of governing, there was peace and no terrorist attacks. This was said during the last three weeks of his presidency.

Then there were the burnings and lootings in Sanford, Florida; Ferguson, Missouri; Baltimore, Maryland; and Seattle, Washington, after a police officer, white or black, killed a supposed unarmed black youth. But no one mentioned the many black youths killed by gang members in Chicago, POTUS's home town. And POTUS did not mention the fact that an illegal, five to seven times deported back to Mexico, killed a beautiful young American girl who fell into the arms of her father in San Francisco. A law was proposed (Kate's Law) to imprison and deport any illegal who came back after being deported, but shamefully it never passed as of this writing. In fact, Congresswoman Pelosi saw fit to make fun of this law. And POTUS said that the country had come together like never before.

Thousands and thousands of illegals were coming invited into our country, creating havoc in some places and bringing diseases that had been eradicated in this country for years, and POTUS told us that our country was the safest it had been in decades.

POTUS was very unfriendly and unhelpful to the nation of Israel and its prime minister, but he said that he had been closer to Israel than any president before him.

But let us forget all that. It's all too controversial and too depressing. On a much brighter note, changing the topic altogether, he was friendly and forthcoming in the following matter: POTUS called and congratulated a hot girl (shall we call her a hot babe?) who attended a Catholic college, insisted on getting free birth control pills, and declared this to be her civil right. (Why she enrolled in a Catholic college and why they did not throw her out were questions that puzzled me for a long while.) POTUS invited her to the White House and bandied her about, a thing to emulate and admire. This hot girl became such a celebrity that the next candidate for the presidency on the Democratic side, Madam "What Difference Does It Make?" the former secretary of state, invited her to come to the Democratic convention. What an honor—so well earned!

Chapter 12

THE NEXT ELECTION

The smartest woman in the world had already prepared for her candidacy in 2016. She was going around making speeches, making a mint in the process, smiling and ingratiating herself to an adoring public. Never mind her abysmal failure as a senator of New York and secretary of state. She was busy flirting with the illegals and promising that those states that demanded photo identification for voting would no longer be allowed to do so, facilitating illegal voting. Those of us who remembered the Constitution, that unique, beautiful document our forefathers left us, felt buried, dejected, and at a loss as to what to do to get out of this morass.

Hillary proceeded to run for what everyone called the third term of POTUS. She won her nomination by cheating the other candidate, poor old Bernie Sanders, out of his votes, a thing that was leaked by our gentle hero WikiLeaks. WikiLeaks also let it be known that the debates questions were given to her beforehand, and she was told to provide questions to ask the Republican candidate. (Was that not nice?)

During the campaign, it came out that she had used a private e-mail server for classified information. She was interrogated for this, and it came out further that there were more than thirty thousand e-mails missing. She invariably said 1) she never used e-mails for her work; 2) she never used that server for classified e-mail—it was just for private use; 3) she only used one server for convenience; 4) none of her e-mails could have been hacked; 5) she never wiped the iPhone off with a cloth; 6) she did not know which information was classified because she never was told how to tell what was classified; and 8) she gave the government all the e-mails it asked for.

(This reminds me of my father's favorite joke. A man borrowed a bowl from his neighbor and never gave it back. When the neighbor finally asked for it back, the man said 1) I never borrowed a bowl from you; 2) it was broken when you gave it to me; and 3) I gave it back to you all shiny and clean three weeks ago. Of course, you had to be there to get the full impact because my father would be laughing all throughout the telling.)

Then it was leaked that Madam Secretary of State had acid-washed the e-mails to erase them (a method to erase e-mails permanently, also called Bleach Bit) and had used a hammer to smash some thirteen iPhones and other devices, though she had clearly sworn that she only owned one. Yet she was never indicted because shortly before the attorney general, Loretta Lynch, good friend of the Clintons, was supposed to hear the case. She was visited by good old Will in an airplane on a tarmac in Phoenix, Arizona, where she was parked for a trip. They discussed their grandchildren and golf games for thirty minutes. After that there was no indictment, but it came out that the attorney general was promised a nice job in the upcoming Hillary Clinton's new administration.

In addition, a congressional committee interrogated the FBI chairman. He told them that what Hillary said was mainly untrue. She had been very careless with her e-mails. But no prosecutor would issue an indictment, as it was not willful. So, it was his recommendation to forget about it.

A lot more stuff came out later about her best friend and confidant, Huma Abedin, a Muslim from a family in Saudi Arabia whose members were all active in the Muslim Brotherhood. Huma had access to all Mrs. Clinton's e-mails, and she even had transferred them to her estranged and very strange husband's computer. Huma has now filed for divorce because her husband's behavior has landed him in jail. But it looks like the so-called lost e-mails will be found on that husband's computer. We will see what the new administration will do with all these goodies.

Chapter 13

THE FINAL DAYS OF OBAMA'S TERM
IN THE WHITE HOUSE

POTUS, meanwhile, had made great strides in freeing terrorists from Guantanamo Bay. He busily freed criminals from American jails so they could vote and commuted sentences for others so they, too, could vote. Before all that, he went to Cuba and reestablished relations with the Castro brothers and allowed trade to commence without stipulating anything good for the people of Cuba, who have been repressed for a long time.

Close to the time his eight years were up, POTUS became very busy. It was time to finish his job while helping Hillary Clinton win the election and showing her the way to follow in his footsteps. There was the matter of letting many more illegals into the country and distributing them in the red states so there would be diversity and a voting bloc of Democrats to balance out the pesky Republicans in the near future (Peter Kirsanov in National Review on February 16, 2015; Allison Graves in PunditFact, November 18, 2016; Steven A. Camarota, Center of Immigration Studies, July 20, 2015.) License plates and licenses were distributed to these illegals so they could get around and vote. They were paid a sum of money so they could get started and vote. They were given cell phones so they could communicate and tell their friends to vote. It was a super arrangement.

Our busy president also arranged to have sixteen different agencies share the material that had accumulated in Utah. Spying on Americans was at an all-time high, perhaps making sure that interested parties knew what the opposition candidate was up to.

Finally, he ensured that Israel once and for all was paralyzed and undercut, so it would never become a peaceful nation. At a meeting in Paris he declared that he was in favor of recognizing a state for the Palestinians, who still maintained that Israel had no right to exist and, in fact, should be wiped off the face of the earth.

A REVIEW OF THE STATE OUR LAST POTUS LEFT US IN

Let us then review what we were left with after the eight years of his administration and what the next president would have to contend with:

1) To help out the world order and fix Israel once and for all, his second secretary of state was sent to Iran to make a peace deal with them. Its final outcome was a series of promises on our part that Iran could make any number of atomic bombs it pleased in fifteen years. In the meantime, it could continue to run the centrifuges to prepare the uranium, some of which they got from the Russians, who got them from US mines Lady "What Difference Does It Make?" sold the Russians under the pay-to-play deal (see "Clinton Cash", by Peter Schweizer, HarperCollins, New York, 2015, 39--57) and under the purview of the Clinton foundation.

2) ISIS is killing, maiming, and trafficking women and inspiring the disaffected youth of the world to commit murder and mayhem.

3) Syria continues to kill at will.

4) Our well-advertised weakness around the world has emboldened North Korea to advance its nuclear arsenal and build long-range intercontinental ballistic missiles, ship-to-ship missiles, and surface-to-ship missiles. North Korea continues to threaten us and the rest of the globe, sharing this weapon technology with Iran.

5) Due to the porous border, there is a continuous influx of illegal Mexicans, Central Americans, South Americans, Syrians, Libyans, and whoever wishes to destroy us from within.

6) We are left unprotected from cyber destruction and electromagnetic pulse attack. POTUS was warned repeatedly that we were in danger from such forces.

7) While our beloved President John F. Kennedy put a man on the moon, the last POTUS, by executive order, put men into girls' bathrooms and vice-versa.

8) He has destroyed the minds of millions of young, middle-aged, and old inhabitants of this nation by turning them into robots, lacking any reasoning power and the ability to see facts.

This last point is evident from the things that come out of the mouths of the Democrats. It is as if a bacterium or virus has been passed around specific to Democrats that has destroyed their brains. They have lost their capacity to think, reason, or understand.

For example, Democrats said that 1) ISIS is not a Muslim problem, 2) climate change is at the base of terrorism, 3) terrorism can be defeated by jobs and love, 4) unemployment insurance is the creator of jobs, and 5) you have to pass a bill before you can read it. A lot of other such nonsense comes out of that party's mouths; that is only the hors d'oeuvre of what has come out of their mouths while our patriotic president was running his campaign and even more so once our new president was elected.

A CONVERSATION AND INTERACTION WITH AN INTELLIGENT WOMAN DEMOCRAT

I had an experience with a Democrat I will never forget. Knowing that she was a Democrat but also caring about this friend, I tried to influence her by giving some simple facts. I begged her to see the movie *Hillary's America* by telling her to do me this one favor. I would reimburse her for the cost. If she was going to vote for Hillary, she should really know something about her, and this was just a short film. Her answer was to unfriend me on Facebook.

I then begged a professor of history to please try to speak to her, as I thought his reasoning would be more erudite and compelling than mine. He wrote her the following letter:

Someone asked a woman how she could vote for Trump, a so-called misogynist, racist and bigot, her answer was:

because I use my head to research and find out what candidates really are all about and not what the media wants me to think;

because Trump has more women in executive and managerial positions than any comparable company, which tells me he is not a misogynist;

because he pays these women the same or more than their male counterparts, which tells me he looks for capacity and skill in people and not color, gender or race;

because he raised wonderful children, who have turned out to be outstanding, hard-working, and compassionate adults;

because his economic plans make sense and are fiscally conservative, I vote for what is best for my family, my friends and my country;

because I fear for my family's safety, if the blatant terrorism continues; it is a direct threat to our way of life;

because it is about someone who puts America first;

because I know he recognizes and embraces American exceptionalism, he will not tour the world, apologizing for who we are, he is a patriot;

because, unlike Mrs. Clinton, he has held a job, built a business, worked hard, created many jobs and achieved success; lastly

because I am more offended by what Hillary does than what Trump says.

My friend's answer to this letter was this:

Take me off your e-mail list. Trump is a racist, misogynist, sexist, evil liar, who is responsible for countless people's misery. You are a complete moron for sending this.

I am a woman and I will never share this view portrayed in this e-mail. Hillary Rodham Clinton is the best and I can't wait to celebrate her BIG WIN!!!!

Can this even be believed? A smart adult person knows nothing about the candidate, absolutely nothing, refuses to watch the movie I had recommended, never read a book about her, though there are many available, is only informed by MSNBC, CNN, the Huffington Post, and the *New York Times*, and obviously spouts back the mantra of the liberal media. It is shameful, pitiful, sad, and dangerous.

From my friend's answer above, I finally realized that the Democrats have an incurable mental condition.

Back to the topic at hand.

Finally, before he went on his vacation, he schemed, planned, and put in place a shadow government that would stop all that our new president intended to do for our country and its legitimate citizens. That was his final coup—that we know of. What else lurks in his plans? I am sure there is much. Only the shadow knows.

Chapter 14

A NEW DAY

As a big inauguration present to our new president, who was elected fair and square by very hard work; a true miracle; and our good, patriotic, grassroot American citizens, Mr. Obama left a country totally divided with irreconcilable differences. The other party was prepared (cooked, recooked, and skewered) by the media and the last administration so that when the next president took office, they refused to recognize him, called him illegitimate, and swore to oppose him in every way they could. Evil billionaires paid troublemakers' salaries, airfares to DC, and hotel accommodations to create protests, hinder traffic, and cause any kind of trouble they could. Since these people were paid to protest and had no idea why they were protesting, they felt no compunctions or restraint.

When the big day came, the day I and millions of patriots, good, decent citizens, the American people (as I know them) had anxiously awaited and eagerly anticipated, the streets in DC were filled with protesters; the seats reserved for Democratic members of congress were empty. Those people were mourning their candidate's loss, their loss of power, their loss of creating a country that not one of us Americans could have recognized by any stretch of our imagination.

Chapter 15

THE CANDIDATE OF THE OPPOSITION PARTY

It is incumbent upon us to see what this other candidate would have brought with her. It is time to study this other side, this Democratic dream that was left unfulfilled by a miraculous act and helped us elect our current president.

All her life, she had wanted to be president. All her life she had craved power. For a thesis in college, she chose to write about Saul Alinsky. She actually met him, was thrilled with him, and learned all about his *Rules for Radicals*. She internalized it and made it her bible, her way to live and move forward, and she has never strayed from it. I could almost grow poetic about this adulation. But let me get back to the topic. Hillary tried her wings as the First Lady of Arkansas, establishing herself as a supporter of women and children's rights. She was actually able to create a childcare system. It was her first crowning achievement. As First Lady of the nation, she went right to work to create an all-encompassing, health-care system for the country (similar to Obamacare), her contribution to the messes her husband indulged in. But the folks at that time (Democrats included) were still in their right minds, so it was nixed forthwith. She then stood firm with her husband and defended him vigorously from all those pesky women with whom he was supposed to have had flings. She especially defended him from that awful young aide, the one with the blue dress and the cigars thrilling her in the Oval Office. ("The Clintons' War on Women" Roger Stone and Robert Morrow, Skyhorse Publ. New York, 2015, 195.) Hillary made sure that her literary prowess was stopped at the beginning while the young thing was attempting to publish a memoir. Her husband, Bill, still almost got impeached and lost his license to practice law for a while. No matter, things were copacetic.

You might want to know what happened next, so we will fast forward.

Hillary became senator of New York in carpetbagger fashion, and we did not hear anything about any accomplishments there. It was a quiet preparation for bigger things to come. She became secretary of state next.

At the same time, Mrs. Clinton was a full partner of a charitable foundation that had supplied much charity to the one that, by adage, warranted charity first: "Charity begins at home." She firmly believed in that saying. So, let us see where the money that was deposited in the foundation's kitty came from. I have, to the best of my ability, summarized it thusly: the money deposited in the Clinton Foundation came from Russia, India, the United Arab Emirates, Saudi Arabia, Kuwait, Uzbekistan, Kazakhstan, China, Cyprus, Mozambique, Senegal, Uganda, Gaza, Algeria, Iran, Sudan, Congo, Ethiopia, Mauritania, Ghana, Nigeria, Colombia, Brazil, Honduras, Belarus, Longo, and Canada.

You have to forgive me if I omitted some countries. These things are foreign to me, and I am having trouble with the correct spelling, let alone finding them on the map. You may ask why these exotic places gave money to this foundation. Was it out of the goodness of their hearts? I would have to say, "No, it was money earned fair and square by the former senator of New York and Madam Secretary of State of the United States while she was in office. In that capacity, but on the side, she was busy doing something good for all those countries and others."

To repeat, she was a very busy lady while in office, but she helped out all those places while doing the job POTUS had appointed her to do. And, yes, I often wondered how she had time for all this extra work, but, you know, a charitable heart can really do wonders. Some people called it pay for play, but I am inclined to dislike this phrase, as there was absolutely no play involved. It was all serious business in that it was a base laid down, carefully, to be continued while she had the ultimate power as president of the United…well, we can't call it States. We would have to call it president of the United Corruptions.

Two egregious things need to be pointed out, resulting directly from the Clinton Foundation. Madam Secretary sold 20 percent of our US uranium mine to the Russians for their atomic bombs. And the Clintons collected $16.4 million to help Haiti after the earthquake hit and destroyed most everything in some areas there. Only 10 percent of the money collected for the express purpose of helping Haiti reached the country; the rest was kept for that proverbial charity at home. In addition, as a side benefit, the Clintons invited their respective brothers to make a killing from directing the reconstructions and to mine Haiti's widely known mineral deposits, including gold and silver mines.

It is no wonder that on the night of the election, according to Larry Schweikart, she was "weeping and crying uncontrollably, she could not stop crying," "became physically violent toward her campaign manager," and screamed psychotically about Russia ("How Trump Won" by Joel B. Pollack & Larry Schweikart. Regnery: Washington, DC, 2017, 204.) She must have remembered all that hard work she had done in all those foreign places, so far away, and now it would all be for naught.

There is also the other matter to talk about, her campaign promises of eliminating the coal industry and all the other antiquated energy producers, increasing taxes, allowing illegals to get voting rights everywhere, and having wide-open, beautiful borders. Yes, wide-open borders would be charitable to all people, whether they wanted to murder us or not—*what difference does it make?*

A few words about the Democratic convention are also in order. I remember the focal points only: that Muslim gentleman with his covered-up wife on his side, silent, as she was supposed to be, who had lost a son in the recent war, waving a booklet around and asking if the other candidate knew a single word of the enclosed Constitution. That was such a moving picture. I don't think I remember much more of that convention except the embracing and happy waving of arms and good old Will taking a nap while the candidate was talking.

Chapter 16

BACK TO THE PRESENT

It has now been almost six months since our president was inaugurated. He still has not been able to close the southern border because the Democrats say that it is un-American not to let ourselves be slaughtered as the British were recently in Manchester and London. The mayors of the sanctuary cities around the country are doubling down and making sure to disobey the orders our president has tried to enforce against allowing criminal illegals to be protected.

President Trump's recent trip to Saudi Arabia, Israel, the Vatican, Belgium, and Sicily was a groundbreaking, humongous success. While I have filled my Facebook page with pictures and videos and could not get enough of them, the Democrats do not know about it because the mainstream media, that monument of truth, barely reported on it.

I have videos of the beautiful greetings President Trump got in Saudi Arabia, with the longest red carpet ever connecting *Air Force One* with the king of the Saudis; the magnificent horse riders in formation; the beautiful water fountains dancing almost to the tempo of the trotting horses; the solemn greetings in the richly decorated palace; and the many Arab leaders in their interesting garbs. I have President Trump going up to the Western Wall in Israel, the remains of the second Jewish temple, saying a prayer and sticking a piece of paper in between the old stones to ask for peace. I have a chatty Sara Netanyahu, not able to contain herself, so eager to talk to our classy First Lady, and the prime minister of Israel with a grin from ear to ear, unable to hide his joy and appear solemn and serious. I have a picture of President and Mrs. Trump visiting a fourteen-year-old girl in Israel who has struggled with cancer for the past seven years and whose wish it was to see our president. And I have Pope Francis, at first serious and stiff, but with a kind smile on his face after he talked to our president. These are pictures and videos for me to view again and again.

Those Democrats are losing all this splendor and pride they could have enjoyed and for what? I ask myself that question often and truly cannot come up with a reasonable answer.

Chapter 17

THE OTHER PARTY AFTER THE ELECTION,
OR "THE RUSSIANS ARE COMING;
THE RUSSIANS ARE COMING"

The Democrats and their representatives and senators have gotten hold of some material leaked by several leftover hate-filled snoops in the White House and are all screaming about Russia and saying we have to investigate Trump and his close advisors colluding with Russia while running his campaign and during the transition before the inauguration. They have taken hold of this Russia saga like a tenacious mastiff holding on to the proverbial postman's pants, and they will not let go. This is after they yelled about impeachment. (It is a puzzlement how they were yelling about impeachment before the man had even laid eyes on the White House or done a blessed thing.) It is now up to a special prosecutor to find out how our president has colluded with Russia and what it resulted in. I bet that the Democrats will manufacture something rare and juicy to report.

After Trump fired the head of the FBI—who had given a pass to the other candidate, as mentioned before, and was now trying his best to implicate friends of the president in collusion with Russia—a big hullabaloo arose. The media screamed, "Russia" some more.

Well, lo and behold, the Senate Intelligence Committee interrogated the former director of the FBI, James Comey, about the Russian collusion under oath. Many Democrats took off from work to be able to watch the scalping of our president; many bars resplendent with big TVs were crowded with watchers. But the answers from Comey completely exonerated and vindicated our president and his consultants from any collusion with Russia. Instead Comey dug himself into a big hole of lying and leaking to the press. He implicated the former attorney general in shady deals and being part of the Clinton clan. It was a disaster of sorts for the former director and an entirely new chapter for the Republicans and the new administration to investigate.

That afternoon there was an eerie silence among the Democrats, but the next day they found a new thing to hang their hats on: obstruction. One of the things Comey had remarked was that our president had said he hoped that he would not bother his friend General Michael Flynn anymore, as the Democrats had managed to destroy the man's career already by innuendos of Russian collusion. The Democrats, after some long deliberations and night musings, called the word *hope* attempted obstruction of justice. And so MSNBC, ABC, and CNN had a reprieve. The next morning, they were all yelling about obstruction of justice.

It is hopeless. As I proved before, they are all infected with a disease. They have nothing else in their repertoire of news except stopping our president from pursuing his work and draining the swamp, which just got swampier.

The Democrats, now, got a hold of a story about one of the sons of President Trump, having had a phony conversation with a lawyer from Russia, promising to give him some dirt about Hillary. At first, he was not interested, but with urging from an acquaintance, listened to her for twenty minutes, after some months, and found out the whole thing was a ruse, to supposedly reinstate adoptions of Russian babies by Americans, which had been forbidden. This set-up is now enough to call him a traitor, colluder, ready to be jailed or better yet shot, and for our President to be held responsible, investigated, and who knows what. It is currently filling the main stream media news to prevent our President to do his job some more. It is the progressive, leftist, liberal ideologues' best work to date. Is this concoction for real? How do you spell entrapment?

Yet the leaked news of Obama and his minions wiretapping, bugging, and hacking all the conversations in Trump Tower and everywhere else to know what Mr. Trump and his confidants were up to did not matter, was OK, and somehow was forgotten. It is infuriating.

ONE MORE THING
The Democrats have a new topic to pursue in addition to obstruction. Our president has kept another promise he made to us deplorables and has gotten us out of the Paris Accord. The leaders of that party are yelling, "Thousands of children are going to die." They say we are a shame to society and other such nonsense. This treaty was to fleece America of billions of dollars to arrange for the prevention of global warming while those countries that polluted the most were not obliged to pay. It was a total farce, yet now the mayors of many cities here have declared that they will not abide by our president's decision and keep the treaty intact. I say let them pay; they should go ahead and pay from their pockets and from the taxes of the citizens who were ignorant enough to elect them. The governor of California has gone to China to deal with them directly to stay in the Paris Accord. I say it is time for California to secede from our country and proudly go it alone.

A PREDICTABLE RESULT

There is no end in sight. It sure looks like Obama has insured that we will never have America again. The mainstream media is continuing its expressions of hatred. Celebrities performed a Shakespeare play in Central Park in New York City, *Julius Caesar*; however, the character being murdered looked much like our president. A so-called female comedian showed herself in a photo on the Internet with the bloodied head of a likeness of our president, reminiscent of an ISIS beheading. Another celebrity announced that she was dreaming of blowing up the White House. So, the insanity continues unabated, inciting the crazies.

On the night before a baseball game in Alexandria, Virginia, between the Republican and Democratic members of Congress, a yearly tradition, the Republicans were practicing. Along came a crazy and shot two representatives and one aide after determining the party the congress people were from. Two policemen were shot, too, but while injured, they were able to take the crazy out.

The majority whip was in critical condition, shot by a rifle that cracked both his hips and injured organs and arteries. I lay this squarely at the feet of the Democrats, their leaders, and the mainstream media. None of them have come forward to say one word except that they hate Trump.

Chapter 18

MY FRIENDS THE REPUBLICANS

And then there is the Republican Congress, which includes RINOS (Republicans in name only), Never-Trumpers (those who did not vote for Trump), and Prima Donnas (those who feel they are the smart ones). They are supposed to have a free and clear way now to pass the laws our president has promised us, namely, to repeal and replace that unaffordable health-care law; lower taxes on businesses, farmers, and others so the country can prosper; and appropriate money to build the wall and fix the infrastructure of this land. But, no, they are dragging their feet, are divided in mission, and are taking vacations instead of working and helping make this country great again. Do they worry about losing power and money, too? Is the status quo what they want? Do they just want to throw their weight around and collect money from lobbyists who want open borders, Obamacare, and no tax changes so they can continue in their corrupt ways, collect their salaries, and keep their jobs? I am puzzled once more. But I have no recourse but to trust our president, who has done so much already, to get things done and keep all the promises he made to us, the American people, the good, the great grassroots of our land.

EPILOGUE

Once there was a land that was the envy of the world. It was a shining example of democracy. It was created as a refuge for people who were persecuted for their religion and who were tired of being taxed by big governments; their freedoms had been curtailed, and they felt oppressed. The group who first established this fairyland had to take a long ocean voyage and go through many privations to establish themselves in this new place. But they were courageous, and they persevered because they longed to be free. They managed to disentangle themselves from the forces that tried to hold them suppressed even in that faraway land. With some wise leaders, they established a government of their own with clever laws that included checks and balances that had never existed before. They called it the US Constitution. It was an amazing piece of legislation. It provided a government for the people, by the people, assured peace and tranquility, and gave everyone the chance to follow their dreams, grow, and be prosperous according to their abilities. It even had provisions to make meaningful changes if enough legislators, carefully described in the plan, agreed to them.

Will we get back to that blessed golden land I came to after ten long years of yearning? Is President Trump strong enough? Does he have enough stamina, enough courage to continue to fight those evil forces that try to stop his every step, his every move, his every breath? I will pray that he does, I will pray that he stays safe, and I will pray that our American patriots will be strong enough to help him drain the swamp and return our country to **America the Beautiful.**

BIBLIOGRAPHY

Alinsky, Saul. 1971. *Rules for Radicals.* New York: Random House.

Altura, Bella T. 2014. *Golden America.* New York: Page.

Beck, Glenn. 2010. *Broke.* New York: Mercury Radio Arts.

Coulter, Ann. 2007. *If Democrats Had Any Brains, They'd Be Republicans.* New York: Crown Forum.

———. 2011. *Demonic.* New York: Crown Forum.

———. 2016. *In Trump We Trust.* New York: Sentinel.

Crowley, Monica. 2012. *What the (Bleep) Just Happened?* New York: Broadside Books.

D'Souza, Dinesh. 2012. *Obama's America.* Washington, DC: Regnery Publishing.

———. 2012. *Unmaking the American Dream.* Washington, DC: Regnery Publishing.

———. 2014. *America.* Washington, DC: Regnery Publishing.

———. 2015. *Stealing America.* New York: Broadside Books.

———. 2016. *Hillary's America.* Washington, DC: Regnery Publishing.

Gingrich, Newt. 2017. *Understanding Trump.* New York: Center Street.

Goss, F.C. *2017. A Deplorable's Confession*. Morehead, KY: Pawprints Publishing.

Hannity, Sean. 2010. *Conservative Victory*. New York: Harper.

Horowitz, David. 2017. *Big Agenda*. West Palm Beach, FL: Humanix Books.

Ingraham, Laura. 2007. *The Power of the People*. Washington, DC: Regnery Publishing.

Limbaugh, David. 2010. *Crimes against Liberty*. Washington, DC: Regnery Publishing.

————. *The Great Destroyer*. 2012. Washington, DC: Regnery Publishing.

Malkin, Michelle. 2009. *Culture of Corruption*. Washington, DC: Regnery Publishing.

Morris, Dick, and Eileen McGann.*2016. Armageddon*. West Palm Beach, FL: Humanix Books.

Pollak, Joel B., and Larry Schweikart. 2017. *How Trump Won*. Washington, DC: Regnery Publishing.

Savage, Michael. 2017. *Trump's War*. New York: Center Street.

Schweizer, Peter. 2015. *Clinton Cash*. New York: HarperCollins.

Stone, Roger, and Robert Morrow. 2015. *The Clintons' War on Women*. New York: Skyhorse.

ACKNOWLEDGMENTS

I would like to thank Burt for fifty-five years of sticking by and supporting me. I would like to thank President Trump for running this arduous campaign and having the stamina and wisdom to get himself elected. I would like to thank Sean Hannity for unceasingly informing me with the truth, and I would like to thank my good friends on Facebook for having kept me from despair those many months of the painful and difficult campaign. Last but not least, I would like to thank all those wonderful Americans who helped make the miracle of this election happen.

APPENDIX

"The Snake," Lyrics of a song released by Al Wilson in 1968, written by Oscar Brown in 1963: "A tender-hearted woman saw a poor half-frozen snake…"